Lifebalance

Balancing work with family and personal needs
(*priority balance*)

Balancing structure with spontaneity
(*attitude balance*)

Balancing achievements with relationships
(*goal balance*)

LINDA AND
RICHARD EYRE

A FIRESIDE BOOK
PUBLISHED BY SIMON & SCHUSTER

FIRESIDE
Rockefeller Center
1230 Avenue of the Americas
New York, NY 10020

First Fireside Edition 1997

FIRESIDE and colophon are registered trademarks
of Simon & Schuster Inc.

Designed by Irving Perkins Associates

Manufactured in the United States of America

10   9   8   7   6   5   4   3   2   1

Library of Congress Cataloging-in-Publication Data

Eyre, Linda.
    Lifebalance : balancing work with family, balancing structure with
spontaneity, balancing achievements with relationships / Linda and
Richard Eyre.—1st ed.
        p.   cm.
    Includes bibliographical references.
    1. Life skills—United States.   2. Time management—United
States.   3. Self-actualization (Psychology)   I. Eyre, Richard M.
II. Title.
HQ2039.U6E965   1997
640′.43—dc20
                                                        96-28996
                                                        CIP

ISBN 0-684-81128-6

Acknowledgments to:

- Friends and brothers, such as the Downeys, the Archibalds, the Mackeys, the Stewarts, the Mayfields, the Chris Eyres, and the Petersens, who read the manuscript long before it was balanced
- Corry DeMille and Lia Davis, who retyped it so often that it threatened their own balance
- Our nine children, who are our prime motivators and reasons for wanting to be balanced

Contents

Introduction

Choosing How We Live

As we lecture and speak to groups around the country, we often ask audiences two questions:

#1. "Do you like *where* you live?"
#2. "Do you like *when* you live?"

Certain answers are predictable . . .

Why it's good to live in America:
freedom, opportunity, beauty, convenience, affluence.
Why it's good to live where they are:
people, neighborhoods, settings, community,
amenities, home.

Why it's good to live now:
technology, options, mobility and transportation,
communication,
science, medicine, entertainment and recreation variety.

Why it's *not* good to live here:
social problems—from abuse to addiction, from poverty
to promiscuity, big taxes and big government,

environmental pollution and media pollution,
immorality and amorality.

Why it's *not* good to live now:
there's too much of everything—too many options, needs,
expectations, competition.
People are longing for simplicity, basics, quality.

After discussion, every time, the audience conclusion
(and our conclusion) is that:
For someone who is
self-directed, self-determining, self-discerning,
self-directioning, self-destiny-ing,
here and *now*
are the best-ever place and time to live.
(*choosing,* and *using* the best of an amazing
abundance of alternatives).

But for someone who is other-directed,
who is controlled, compelled, coerced, or conned
by media, materialism, marketing,
and "mainstream morality"
here and *now* are the worst-ever place and time to live.
(better to have been born 100 years ago
in a basic community with built-in
friends and standards, surrounded by
less influences and options).

Now (with all due respect to Dickens)
is the best of times and the worst of times
(and *here* is the best of places and the worst of places)

depending on our powers
of *Selectivity*.

We then ask audiences:
#3. "Do you like *how* you live?"
While on #1 and #2 the positives come out first,
on #3 it's the negatives:
too hectic, too fast-paced, too much to do, too far behind.
Stretched, stressed, strained, stirred-up, strung out,
unsatisfied, unfulfilled, uninspired, unable
to get ahead, get it together, get it done.
Some good moments, but droplets in a sea of discontent—
lives of quiet desperation.

Again, the more we talk, the more apparent it becomes . . .
the solution is *selectivity,* the cure is *choosing*.
Not to get more done but to be more selective about
what we do—
not more quantity but more quality.
We like *how* we live if we *choose* how we live
and we live in a time and place where doing so
is both more possible
and more difficult
than ever before.

Choosing *how* we live . . .
practicing selectivity to allot our finite time, thought,
and energy
among our infinite options, alternatives, and wants
is what we call *Lifebalance*.
Lifebalance is figuring out how to give more of ourselves
to what does matter and less of ourselves to what doesn't.

Lifebalance is "applied selectivity"—choosing how we *act*
on our life options.
And since our *here* and *now* is less predictable
than any other,
Lifebalance is also choosing how we will react
to our nonoptions,
to the things that happen *to* us—that act on us.
Part of Lifebalance is learning to view surprises
as opportunities,
to let spontaneity be as important as structure,
flexibility and diversion as valued
as firmness and discipline.

We have *no* choice over *when* we live
We have *some* choice over *where* we live
We have *ultimate* choice over *how* we live
Lifebalance is choosing how we live
Lifebalance is choosing how we live!

Prologue

As we write, baby boomers are turning fifty! Books about
angels and spirituality and virtues are best-sellers. Simplifying and looking for quality is more in style than accu-
mulating and looking for quantity. Perhaps something
about the proximity of the year 2000 causes personal in-
trospection.

We live in an interesting era. As we approach and enter a
new millennium, life is, as it has always been, a *search*. But
lately what we are searching *for* has changed dramatically.
During this century most Western men and women have
not had to devote so much of themselves to the search for
survival—for basic food, clothing, and shelter, so they have
sought harder for identity, recognition, "success," achievement, position, wealth, and material things. But now, as the
century (and the millennium) ends, more and more of us
are shifting our search once again—looking for (and longing for) more peace, more harmony, more quality in our
lives, more *balance*.

It is an inner search more than an outer one. It has more
to do with what's happening in our minds and hearts than in
our bank accounts or our resumes, and the only way it can
be measured is by the joy we feel in living. It is a search for a
balance of *priorities* between the needs of our work, our
families, and ourselves, a balance of attitudes between the
structure and discipline we all need with the spontaneity
and flexibility we all want; and a balance of our goals

between achievements and relationships, between things and people.

Before we can begin a meaningful search for balance, we need to recognize and acknowledge our *un*balance. This book begins with some "lifescenes"—all-too-typical moments in all-too-typical lives. The reason some of them will seem so familiar is that you may already have lived them.

This is a personal book. Every chapter has a couple of little stories or incidents about our own lives, our own family, our own discoveries and experiences, and our own frustrations and struggles in our personal search for lifebalance. There are also anecdotes from others we've learned from or watched in their own search for balance.

The book is also the story of a journey—our journey toward what we think is a better way to live. We've chosen to put balance ahead of business and quality in front of quantity. It was a choice that took us a while to make, and that involved some interesting trade-offs, such as fewer social gatherings and more kite flying, making fewer "contacts" and more friends, acquiring fewer things and gaining more time, giving up some major clients in order to spend a summer together as a family building a log cabin.

We view ourselves—and invite you to view us—not as experts nor perfect examples of *Lifebalance* but as one case study in the struggle. We're not speaking as those who have arrived and now shout back at you to follow. Rather we've started a journey in a new direction toward a calmer, more balanced place. We invite you to travel with us.

Linda and Richard Eyre
Piea, Maui, 1996

P.S. We hope as you read that this becomes a personal book for you, too. One reason for the wide margins is to give you space to make your own notes and observations about balance—so that when you finish the book, it will contain a lot of "your way" as well as a lot of ours.

THE

Symptoms

Lifescenes

PORTRAITS OF UNBALANCE

Fourteen individuals. A through N, Alan through Nancy, typical transition Americans. Which of them could almost be you?

Alan is exhausted driving home from the airport after a week-long business trip. It's Saturday afternoon and he's anxious to see his family. The two or three weeks before the trip had been so hectic that he was getting home after the kids were in bed every night.

He turns onto his street and sees a small girl playing in his front yard. A friend of his daughter's, he guesses. She looks a little older than his daughter—maybe a new family has moved into the neighborhood. He wonders where Allison is. She must be around, or this little girl wouldn't be here.

It is not until he pulls into the driveway and the girl runs toward the car that he realizes it *is* Allison. How can she have grown that much? He feels a pang of joy as she reaches up to hug him—and then a wave of guilt. For a minute he didn't recognize his own daughter!

Barbara is upwardly mobile, assertive, with much of her identity wrapped up in her position in her firm. She's home from work now but still in her business suit. With her briefcase open on the kitchen table, appointment book in hand, she is trying to finish up some of the calls and E-mail she didn't have time for at the office. She has been interrupted now several times by her four-year-old son, a round-faced little boy with big blue eyes.

"Mom, what's in that big book?"

"This is Mommy's appointment book, Timmy. What's in it are important things I have to do and the names of important people. Now, run upstairs and play with your toys."

Timmy wanders toward the stairway looking dejected. Then his face brightens and he turns back to his mom and tugs on her skirt. She looks down at him and says through clenched teeth, "What *is* it, Timmy?"

"I just wondered, Mommy," Timmy says, his eyes pleading. "Is my name . . . in your book?"

———————

Carol has a love-hate relationship with airplanes. On the one hand they are her only solitude, the only place she is free of people who need her and of things that beg to be done. (She's refused so far to avail herself of incoming or outgoing air phone calls.) On the other hand they keep her from the people she loves and the tasks that pile up while she is away. She'll arrive home Wednesday, a couple of hours before her husband, Charles, leaves on a two-day business trip of his own. At least the kids won't have to be with an overnight sitter this week.

———————

Dave is lacing up his old gym shoes for the first time in months. His doctor didn't mince words yesterday. "Dave, your health has deteriorated since your last checkup. Your weight and your blood pressure are both going in the wrong direction." *Things have been so hectic lately,* Dave thinks, *there seems to be so little time and so much stress. It's definitely time to get back in shape. It won't take that many workouts to get the old body on track again,* he tells himself. *I'm resilient; I can do it.*

Dave has to sit down after a half mile at a slow trot. His knee hurts and his chest is burning. *What's happening to me?* he wonders. *What have I lost, and exactly where did I lose it?*

As the members of the city orchestra begin to tune their instruments, Ellie shifts to the edge of her seat in anticipation. *It's been over a year since I've been to a concert,* she thinks. Unbelievable. Music used to be her life, but there's no time anymore. The music lifts her, changes how her mind works, changes how the world looks.

"Who's the violinist in the third chair? It looks like . . . no, it couldn't be. She works, too—and has children, like I do." Ellie squints and tries to see the woman's face. "It is! She played behind me in the college orchestra. I haven't touched my violin for months—for years, really! How does she keep up? When does she practice?"

Ellie doesn't feel happy for her old friend. She feels resentment. But not at the woman on the stage . . . at herself. She hasn't taken the time to nurture her talent. And her talent is leaving her.

For Faye every evening seems like a nightmare. There's the flurry of calls and needs that keep her at the office later and later, the rush-hour traffic that slows and stops her a dozen times, finally getting home with barely two hours to feed the kids and help with homework before they should be in bed. And then her beeper goes off, and she hears something coming in on the fax, and needs to check her E-mail. Maybe on Saturday there will be some "quality time" with the kids. . . . No, that's Fred's visitation day.

Gordon is sitting on the commuter train next to a wrinkled old family doctor, a general practitioner. Just retired, he's reminiscing about his fifty years of broken bones, vaccinations, checkups, and especially about sitting at the bedsides of people about to die. "You know, it's interesting," the physician says. "You hear a lot of regrets from people on their deathbeds, but I'll tell you one I've never heard. No one ever says, 'If only I'd spent a little more time with the business.' "

Two little, high-pitched voices are trying to outyell each other. Is this a home or a torture chamber?

Heather yells back at her two preschoolers, hoping her demand to "be quiet" will somehow prevail because of its superior decibel level.

It was Heather's choice to stay home with the kids. When she is honest with herself, she realizes it's not her career she misses—well, she does miss work, too—but more than that, it's the *time* she had for herself. She misses getting ready in the morning, looking nice, getting complimented, and being alone once in a while. She misses setting a pencil down and coming back to find it is still there!

Browsing in a bookstore feels like paradise to Ilene. I used to read, she thinks, I really did! And buy books. I knew what the latest ideas were—I got high on vicarious experiences and new theories. It takes energy to read, though. And I don't have any energy left after the job and kids every day. I have to neglect something—I guess I've already chosen what it will be. She puts the book back on the shelf—it's time to pick up the kids.

Jake has two hours on this airplane, and his secretary is waiting at the office for him to fax the memo from the airport so that she can get it to the division head before his New York conference call.

And the person in the next seat wants to talk. A nice enough older lady, rather eccentric-looking. But why can't she see how busy he is? She's asked him three questions, and he's given three one-word answers. Finally she has taken the hint, and is reading a thick, hardbound book— perhaps a biography.

Jake finishes the memo just in time, gets off the plane, and heads for the fax machine. He notices the lady again as he passes the baggage claim and realizes that she is probably a very interesting woman. Jake finds himself vaguely wishing he had time to find out more about people—to talk to them to see how they view the world.

Imagine Ken trying to explain *this* one to the vet: The cat was bitten by the dog because the dog was in a bad temper because he had been kicked by Kevin because Kevin was upset because his mother yelled at him about leaving his coat on the chair because she was irritated because her husband Ken had snapped at her because he felt uptight because his boss had criticized his monthly report because he felt a lot of stress because the company president had called him on the carpet because he was worried because the board had raised the company's sales quota.

There's not enough room on the calendar. There are too few hours in each day, too few days in each week. Larry tries to sit down with his wife to "coordinate schedules," but all they figure out is that their schedules can't coordinate. There are too many meetings and too much work, too many music lessons, too many PTA meetings, too many Little League games, and too many social commitments. They haven't eaten together as a family for two or three weeks. They agree that they're "overcommitted," but they can't agree what to do about it.

Matt and Meg are celebrating their twentieth anniversary. The restaurant is beautiful, everything looks right, but their feelings are flat. There is less intensity in their love, less feeling when their hands touch, less fire—even in their disagreements. But they don't really love each other any less. Surely they don't. It's just that they're both so busy. A good, long talk will put everything right again—won't it?

Nancy thought there were pressures at work! No one understands the pressures on a single parent. Each of the children wants something. There are five dilemmas, three problems, and two conflicts that you are expected to solve. And the toilet ran over again. Coming home is like jumping out of the frying pan and into the fire. Maybe working late would have been a good idea. Maybe another hour or two at day care would have been better for the kids than this.

Crowded Complexity

More "lifescenes" like these are easy to find. They are all around us.

We're all busy people, doing so much, but somehow leaving out the most important things.

People who are tired enough to know they've been working hard yet still not too sure that anything worthwhile is getting done.

People who get their jollies by crossing things off their "to do" list, but who have lost their spontaneity.

People who live to work rather than work to live.

People who are always remembering how it was or thinking about how it will be.

People who read every article they see on stress and depression.

People who want to simplify, get back to the basics, and slow down, but who never get around to doing so (or even figure out how it could be done).

People who are reaching their goals, but wondering if they are the right goals.

People who say they're happy, but can't define happiness and wonder if they even understand the word.

People who are too busy "getting there" to enjoy the journey.

People who see their kids growing up too fast and their own lives going by too fast and feel they're missing the boat in both categories.

❖　❖　❖

In the Western world, before the Industrial Revolution, the prevailing personal challenge was *survival*.

Following the Industrial Revolution the personal challenge was physical and economic *quality of life*.

Today the personal challenge is *balance*.

Because there are so many possibilities and responsibilities, so many options, alternatives, choices, it's hard to balance our *time* and our *priorities*.

Because to be successful we need to be strong and structured; and yet to be fun, we need to be flexible and free, it's hard to balance our *attitudes*.

Because there are so many things we want and so many people who need us or whom we care for, it's hard to balance our *goals*.

We have the same amount of mental energy and the same number of hours in a day as people of other generations and other locations, but we have so many more demands on us.

We live in the first time and place in the world's history and geography where our challenges stem not from scarcity but from surplus, not from oppression but from options, and not from absence but from abundance.

Instead of struggling to find our next meal, we are struggling to get our busy families together long enough to eat a meal. Instead of searching for information, we are buried in it. Instead of striving for the connections of communication and being in touch, we long for the privacy of escaping or disconnecting the technology that makes us always accessible, always available. Instead of fighting for freedom to make our own choices, we are reeling in the abundance of our options . . . 250 TV channels, 500 new Internet sites every day, tens of thousands of consumer items, and almost

limitless numbers of education, job, and lifestyle alternatives.

*It's not the sparse simplicity of too little but the crowded
complexity of too much that plagues our lives. And the
answers lie not in the balance of our abilities but in our
ability to balance.*

A Warning and a Promise

Definition

Lifebalance is the art of balancing such *finite* things as our time, our energy, and our thought among the seemingly *infinite* needs of our work, our families, and our personal interests and obligations.

Lifebalance also means the balance of our attitudes and approaches to life between the structured and the spontaneous, between fixed schedules and flexibility, between our needs to be plugged in and our needs for privacy.

And finally, it implies balancing achievements with relationships, things with people, "getting" with "being."

Lifebalance involves doing something about our priorities and asking ourselves some hard questions about what really matters and about whether we are living our lives accordingly.

Balancing, for most of us, sounds like a pretty good idea (and a very real need). But there is a warning that ought to come first, a factor you ought to consider before you adopt the goal of Lifebalance—something you should ponder before you even decide to read the rest of this book.

Warning

People who live balanced lives may be less likely to have a bridge or a park or a fountain or a monument named after them. They may have less chance of becoming a solo artist with the Boston Philharmonic or of winning the Nobel Prize for Science. They are probably less likely to become U.S. senators or to form massive financial or business empires. And they may not use or avail themselves of every single new technology or every bit of available new information.

It is not impossible for balanced people to do these things, but they are less likely to do them than *single-minded* people who pursue them with all their time and resources and energy.

In our new world, the accepted route to success (in fact the accepted *definition* of success) is narrow specialization. The broad "Renaissance man" (or woman) isn't found much anymore as an ideal or even as an idea.

If your goal is to get a bridge named after you, read a different book. But if you are occasionally touched by the vivid realization that this body and mind are the only ones you will ever develop, that this family is the only one you will ever raise, that this earth is the only one you will ever live on, that this life is the only one you will ever live (and that it is too short either to waste or to spend on one thing at the expense of everything else), then you are reading the right book, and we welcome you to the idea and the solution and the system of Lifebalance.

And come to think of it, there is something of a backlash building up in our world against specialization and against directing all we have to narrow careers that force us into knowing more and more about less and less. It is a backlash against the whole idea of living to work instead of working to live; against the stress and competitiveness of our urban, technological, materialistic society; and against the notion of forfeiting our bodies and our souls and our families for something that the world mistakenly calls success.

So who knows—the world may be changing, and may once again name its bridges after balanced men and balanced women.

And if our children and our friends don't put our names on monuments, they may nonetheless put our examples into their lives and our memories into their hearts.

Culprits

When unbalance occurs in a circus, it is very easy to see. The man on the high wire slips, loses his confidence, begins to wobble, and in the audience our hearts jump into our throats. When the juggler loses his concentration, he drops one ball and haplessly tries to catch the others as they fall out of orbit. We look away, embarrassed for him.

In life, unbalance is a little harder to see. People become rather good at hiding the stress and frustration they feel. They conceal the worry that things aren't right in their families and the fact that they are neglecting crucial things, such as their own bodies, their own minds, and their own children, in favor of less crucial things, such as social ladders and career ladders.

But we don't hide our unbalance from ourselves. Thoreau said (even before beepers, fast food, and the Internet) that most men live "lives of quiet desperation." Whether we call it desperation or information overload, we know our lives are at least a little out of balance. Some of us are so painfully aware of our unbalance that we think Thoreau's description was an understatement. Others of us occasionally long for a little more solitude, more time to think, more time to relax with our families, or simply for a slower, more flexible, more private, more meaningful lifestyle. And sometimes, in the pure joy of a spontaneous moment or an unexpected brand-new friendship, we stop and wonder why it doesn't happen to us more often. We feel creative urges, emotional tugs, adventuresome parts of us stirring within, but there's no time for them—there isn't even time for the things we have to do.

When stress, frustration, or exhaustion remind us that we are out of balance, whom do we blame?

When the tightrope walker slips or the juggler's batons bounce off each other and clatter to the floor, it's pretty easy to find an outside cause. Maybe the tightrope was loose or a baton was slippery; perhaps a camera flash distracted the performer, or maybe there was even a slight earth tremor.

And maybe there's an external explanation for our own unbalanced lives. After all, our parents and grandparents didn't feel the stress that we do, so it must be something in our world.

Here's a list of potential culprits:

- Too many options (too much to do)
- Advertising, materialism (too much to want)
- Competitive expectations (too much to become)
- Excessive technology (too many connections, too little privacy)
- All of the above

Which one is it? None of the above! Unbalance may *seem* to be a product of the world around us, but we actually cause it ourselves—by the choices we make, the way we live, the way we plan, the way we think.

Samuel Johnson put it very succinctly: "He who has so little knowledge of human nature as to seek happiness by changing anything but his own disposition will waste his life in fruitless efforts and multiply the grief he proposes to remove."

We talk quite a bit these days about stress, about overload, about emptiness, about unbalance. But our talk is usually just commiseration—about how bad it is, how impossible it is to do anything about it, in that at least we're not alone; everyone feels it.

This book is more than a discussion of the problem. It is an attempt to help you *change* the way you think, and the way you function and balance your life. It will not give you some magic formula for how to do everything at once; on the contrary, it may help more with deciding what *not* to do and what *not* to have. It will suggest some ways to decide what's important and what isn't—and it will suggest a system of planning and of thinking that will keep the important things (and the important parts of ourselves) in balance.

If you simply want to increase the *quantity* of things you get done in a day, almost any planning, scheduling, or time-management program will help.

But if you are more interested in improving the *quality* of the things you do each day, then *Lifebalance* was written for you. Rather than attempting to help you get more done, it will encourage you to do fewer unimportant things in order to do more about the important things in your life.

Promise

You have the capacity to balance yourself, to set your own priorities. Our influence over ourselves can be far stronger than any other influence.

Imagine an iceberg. A gale-force wind is blowing, causing the snow and ice particles on the iceberg to stream horizontally in one direction. Yet the iceberg is moving steadily *in the opposite direction*. The reason is the *current*. The current is less visible than the wind, but far more powerful.

The currents in our lives are generated by our choices. The world with its materialism, information, technology, competitiveness, and busyness may swirl around us, blowing us toward overload, unbalance, and stress; but the currents created by our choices and the habits we choose to develop can propel us in opposite directions, toward the quality of life found in meaningful, prioritized living.

There was once a preschool that had one unit in its curriculum on "goal setting." A four-year-old boy, after hearing some stories that explained the idea of goals to him, decided his goal would be to stop sucking his thumb.

The thumb sucking also involved dragging around a tattered old blanket, which he rubbed with the thumb and forefinger of one hand while sucking the thumb of the other hand. Appropriately, the boy's name was Linus.

The teacher tried to get Linus to think of an easier goal, but he was insistent. He tried for a couple of days without success and then said, "Teacher, I just don't think I'm going to be able to give up my thumb as long as I have the blanket. Here, will you put it up on the refrigerator, where I can't feel it?" With the blanket out of reach, Linus got over his thumb-sucking habit.

Unbalance in our lives results from bad habits—habits that emphasize work at the expense of family and personal growth, or structure at the expense of spontaneity, or accomplishments at the expense of relationships (or vice versa on any of the above).

These bad habits may have to do with the way we think, or with the way we plan or don't plan, or simply with the way we live our lives each day.

To blame our habits of unbalance on the world, or on the materialism or complexity around us, or on the responsibilities and demands on our time would be a lot like blaming the habit of thumb sucking on the blanket.

The blanket may be *contributing* to the problem, and removing the blanket's influence from our lives may help us to change, but the problem is the habit, and we change our habits only by changing ourselves.

Let's look more closely at some of the bad habits that we develop and that tend to unbalance our lives—and at some of the "blankets" which make them hard habits to break:

• Partly because of the "blankets" of peer pressure and competitive specialization, many of us get into the habit of using all our time and mental energy on our work and having none left over for family and personal needs.

• Partly because of the "blankets" of too many responsibilities and the complexity and busyness of our lives, we often get into the habit of relying on too many lists and on so much structure that there is no room for spontaneity or surprises, for flexibility or fun.

• Partly because of the "blankets" of the fast pace of our world and its rampant materialism, most of us get into the habit of not communicating very well about our feelings and of measuring ourselves much more on the quantity of our achievements than on the quality of our relationships.

The next section, called "The Solution," is about getting rid of old "blankets" and old habits and developing some new and more balanced ways of thinking and of looking at life.

The last section, called "The System," is about developing some new habits that will keep the old ones from coming back—and keep the blankets up on the refrigerator.

But solutions are hard to implement or even to find until we have become more specific and more personal about the problem and recognize the specific areas in which we each have balance problems. The two short tests that follow are designed to help you recognize and define your own particular unbalance.

Two Short Balance Tests

In our culture, when you don't feel quite right physically, it's common for the doctor to "take a few tests" before she makes a diagnosis. If you are wondering just *where* your life is out of balance, the following tests may help you to find out. They may prove that there is more unbalance in your life than you had thought, or they may confirm some things you really already knew but hadn't fully admitted to yourself.

Be candid and honest with your answers. These are private tests, and if anyone *corrects* them, it will be you! Let the results illuminate rather than worry you. Remember, unbalance is the norm in our world, and it can't be corrected or controlled until it is discovered or diagnosed.

Test 1

On a blank sheet of paper or on the spaces printed here, prioritize the following four things. Write them in the space below, in order of how much they mean to you, with the most important element listed first.

Work or Career	Personal Character (including beliefs, inner growth, etc.)	Family	Other Interests (including recreation, technology, entertainment, etc.)

1. _____

2. _____

3. _____

4. _____

When you have finished, turn the paper over (or use the margin of this page) and list the same four things again, only this time put them in order of how much *time* and *thought* you spend on each.

Test 2

Go through the following questions in sequence, jotting brief answers in the lines provided or on a separate, numbered sheet of paper. If a question seems hard or obscure or takes too much thought, skip it and go on to the next question. Don't go back to the questions you skipped until you read the paragraphs following the test.

1. What was the most recent advancement, promotion, or raise you received at work?

_____

_____

_____

2. Do you have any written goals for your marriage? (If so, what are they?)

_____

_____

_____

3. Think quickly of a thing you are better at or a way in which you are better off than the neighbors living on each side of you.

_____

_____

_____

4. Think quickly of a new marriage relationship skill or a parenting technique you have discovered or are working on.

_____

_____

_____

5. What is your latest "technology discovery" (the latest thing you have learned about technology or the newest piece of technology you have acquired)?

_____

_____

_____

6. Name the latest discovery you have made about the nature or potential or talent of someone in your immediate family.

_____

_____

_____

7. What are two "achievement goals" you have for this year (two things you would like to accomplish)?

_____

_____

_____

8. Recall the last important discovery you made about yourself.

_____

_____

_____

(continued)

9. What specific five-year goals do you have financially or for your career?

_____

_____

_____

10. What is your latest personal creative effort? (When did you write a poem, paint, etc.?)

_____

_____

_____

11. What are your best skills and abilities at work? What attributes contribute to your success?

_____

_____

_____

12. What are your best skills and most natural ability as a spouse and as a parent?

_____

_____

_____

13. What is the last thing you've read relating to your career or field of work?

_____

_____

_____

14. What are the last two books you've read for relaxation or out of an interest unrelated to your career?

_____

_____

_____

15. Name the three biggest challenges you currently face at work.

_____

_____

_____

16. What are the three most important things you want to give to your children?

_____

_____

_____

17. Whom do you admire most for his or her accomplishments?

_____

_____

_____

18. Whom do you admire most for his or her sensitivity?

_____

_____

_____

(continued)

19. Name the last project you carefully planned and executed.

_____

_____

_____

20. What is the last completely spontaneous thing you can remember doing?

_____

_____

_____

21. Think back over last week. What is the most important thing you accomplished?

_____

_____

_____

22. Think again over the past week. What is the most playful or silly thing you did?

_____

_____

_____

23. What is your favorite time-management or planning system?

_____

_____

_____

24. When did you last participate in an exciting discussion of *ideas* unrelated to your work?

_____

_____

_____

25. What is the last thing you got really excited about doing?

_____

_____

_____

26. When was the last time you felt completely relaxed?

_____

_____

_____

27. When did you last apply "positive mental attitude" to a situation?

_____

_____

_____

28. How many good belly laughs have you enjoyed this week?

_____

_____

_____

(continued)

29. Did you make some lists of things to do this last week and cross them off as you did them?

_____

_____

_____

30. What is the most beautiful aspect of nature you noticed last week?

_____

_____

_____

31. Name the last problem you figured out, analyzed, and solved?

_____

_____

_____

32. When did you last have a "flash insight" or an answer or insight that just seemed to come out of nowhere? What was it?

_____

_____

_____

33. List three or four things that you discipline yourself
to do every day.

_____

_____

_____

34. What was the best question you thought of or pondered this week?

_____

_____

_____

35. What is the most exciting thing you've purchased
lately (your newest possession or "toy")?

_____

_____

_____

36. When is the last time you had a personal spiritual
experience or felt deeply moved by something?

_____

_____

_____

(continued)

37. What is one thing you'd really like to buy right now if you had enough money?

_____

_____

_____

38. Name two people you plan to get to know better simply because they seem like interesting people.

_____

_____

_____

39. What is the latest thing you did (or acquired) in order to be "connected" or to make information available (e.g., beeper, E-mail, Internet, fax)?

_____

_____

_____

40. What is the latest thing you did to provide yourself with more privacy or solitude?

_____

_____

_____

41. What are the things in your wardrobe that you absolutely could not get along without?

_____

_____

_____

42. Name two people who have confided in you lately.

_____

_____

_____

43. Name one or two of the best new business contacts you have made recently.

_____

_____

_____

44. Think of a good friend. What are his or her two biggest needs?

_____

_____

_____

45. Of whom do you feel just a little bit jealous?

_____

_____

_____

46. Who is the most interesting stranger you have had a conversation with lately?

_____

_____

_____

Results and Implications of Test 2

Let's talk about the second test first—the one you just finished. We'll go back to the first test in a moment. On the second (forty-six question) test there are no "right" or "wrong" answers. The real "test" has to do with which questions were easier for you to answer. A quick tip-of-the-tongue answer indicates that you are *oriented* to the subject of that question, that your awareness level of its contents was fairly high.

If you look back over the test, you will realize that the odd-numbered questions have to do with work and career, with structured thinking, and with achievement. The even-numbered questions deal more with family and personal growth, with spontaneity and with relationships.

On the first eighteen questions, if the odd numbers were the easiest to answer, you are more occupied with work and career than with family and personal growth. If the "evens" were easy and the "odds" hard, you may be too family- and character-development-oriented. (You are also a distinct minority.)

On the next sixteen questions (numbers 19–34), easier "odds" point to an unbalance of too much structure and too little spontaneity (and vice versa).

On the last dozen questions (numbers 35–46), easier "odds" suggest you are too achievement-oriented. Easier "evens" (a rarity) indicate that you may be so sensitive and conscious of other people that you don't accomplish much yourself.

Results and Implications of Test 1

As we have used the first test in seminars around the country, a consistent (and somewhat disturbing) pattern has become clear. Most people list their priorities (on the front side) in the following order:

1. Family
2. Personal character
3. Work or career
4. Other interests

Sometimes numbers 1 and 2 are reversed, and sometimes 3 switches with 4. But the majority list them as they appear above.

On the "other side," when listed in order of time and thought spent, the list is often *reversed*.

1 or 2. Work or career
2 or 1. Other interests
3 or 4. Personal character
4 or 3. Family

"Work or career" most often heads this second list, although careful calculation (of time and thought expended) sometimes puts "Other interests" (often over forty hours a week) even higher. Whichever is the winner, one of the two is almost always well ahead of "Personal character" and "Family."

Some might say that the test is unfair—that we *have* to

spend forty or more hours a week working and simply don't have the luxury of putting more important things first. But the disturbing ranking holds even when the *time* measurement is removed and we rank things in order of the *thought* we give them.

So, whatever the reasons are, and wherever the blame rests, the point is that our list of priorities and our list of how we spend our time and our thought are opposites. We know what is most important, but that knowledge does not translate into how we live our lives. And therein lies the well-justified concern that most of us feel about unbalance.

THE

Solution

Three Kinds of Balance

Balance

Is balance another name for art?
Harmonies that merge and meld melodies,
Composition where form complements form and color,
Architecture that seems grown more than built.
What is it about balance that is so appealing?
The gliding stride of a tiger (or a house cat),
The swift, sure, solid steps of a tightrope walker,
The gravity-reduction of a flowing, floating ballerina,
The air-patterns of the juggler's balls,
The tackle-shedding equilibrium of a running back.

There is *peace* in balance, *tranquil, calm.*
The difference between a "9" and a "10"
on the balance beam
Is ease—making the hard look easy.
There is no rush in balance, no stress.
The ball moves in slow motion on the seal's nose,
The hang glider shifts his weight so slightly,
The log turns smoothly, spiked shoes centered.
The element of danger, always there, in fact the *reason,*
Is shrunk by balance.

And with the peace is purpose, passion, power,
A straight spindle, stilled by the spin.

Even beyond the beauty of physical balance
Is balance in the mind,
A peaceful, time-slowing, awareness-growing
Equilibrium of the soul,
With thoughtful juggling of chosen priorities,
So that each is touched regularly, caught and held,
Nothing precious dropped.
With centered mental footwork high on the log
That floats and spins between structure and spontaneity
And with measured mind-weight-transfers
To keep the *things* and *achievements* on one end
of the teeterboard
From bouncing off the *people* and the *relationships*
on the other.

Balance stands out because unbalance is everywhere.
Our world spins perfectly on its axis
But little on it or in it reflects the balance.
Do we want it enough to work for it?
To do the hardest work—which we call *changing*?

Changing:

> How we plan,
> How (and what) we value,
> How we think,
> How we live.
> How we live balance.
> How we lifebalance.

Three Kinds of Balance

There are three kinds of unbalance that plague our lives, three kinds of balancing at which we need to be adept if we want to improve the quality of our lives.

The first we will call *priority balance*—the balance between family, career, and personal growth. It involves an increased awareness of what is important and an ability to balance our thought and our effort *among the things that really matter*. It requires a new way of planning. Not the typical scheduling session where we sit down and ask only one question: "Now, what do I have to *do*?" Rather, *Lifebalance* will suggest a new kind of balanced planning where we also ask ourselves questions like "What do I *choose* to do? or "What *should* I do?" or even "What do I *want* to do?"

The second type of balance is *attitude balance*—the balance between structure and spontaneity. It involves the skill of being both firm and flexible, both disciplined and dreamy. It involves being aware and watching for unanticipated needs and unplanned opportunities, and it requires some serendipity to go along with our schedules. *Lifebalance* will propose a form of balanced planning that welcomes and enhances the *unplanned*.

The third kind of balance is *goal balance*—the balance between achievements and relationships, between people and things. Lifebalance involves setting aside specific time for communicating, for listening, for understanding, and it introduces a new kind of objectives, called relationship goals, which are quite different from the achievement goals we are more accustomed to.

To fix these three kinds of balance in our minds, let's go back to our circus analogy. Imagine a three-ring circus. In one ring is the juggler, keeping all his balls in the air. In the second ring is the tightrope walker, and in the third a teeter-totter, where the acrobats on one side bounce and balance those on the other.

Now imagine the three rings of Lifebalance. Priority balance is in the first ring. It's a matter of selecting which balls are important and then gaining the skill to keep them all in the air at once. Attitude balance, in the second ring, is a matter of staying upright on life's rope by not slipping too far toward the structure nor too far toward the spontaneity side. Goal balance, in the third ring, requires enough weight on the relationship side of the teeter-totter to counterweigh the efforts we make on the achievement side.

Why-To and How-To

Learning to balance priorities, attitudes, and goals is an individual process. Each formula is unique because each person and set of circumstances is unique. But the principles are the same, and the motivations are similar.

Ideas, methods, techniques, and other how-tos are helpful, sometimes because they work for you "as is" and other times because they trigger a more personally tailored idea of your own.

Often, the why-tos are even more important. As people are motivated and commit themselves to better balance, as they want it more and understand more why they need it, they discover and design personal how-tos that are far better for themselves than ideas suggested by or borrowed from others. The sections that follow are a collection of *principles* that always apply; of ideas or methods that sometimes apply and that sometimes prompt related, similar ideas; and of illustrations and arguments that build the cause and the motivation for making stronger efforts at Lifebalance.

Priority Balance

BALANCING WORK WITH FAMILY WITH SELF

Priorities

Priorities
More a word used than a principle practiced.
Easy to discuss, to agree,
Hard to do, to apply.
Priorities often stand like
Stoic sentries,
Simple to meet, but distant, hard to get to know.
Pull priorities closer, into the firelit center
Of mental focus.
Be selective about who is drawn in
And treat each invited guest as a sovereign.

Wishing

Conceptually, priorities are simple, even obvious. We *should* know what is important to us, and we *should* spend our time and our thought on the high priorities rather than the low ones.

But in reality, in the day-to-day, it is not so simple. As the tests on pages 36–47 pointed out, there is often little correlation between how important things are to us and how much thought or effort we give to them. We constantly find ourselves wishing we had time for the really important things, wishing there were more hours in the day, wishing life were less complex, and wishing we were better at juggling all the things we need to do.

The principles of this priority-balance section are intended to help you stop wishing and start changing.

Simplification and Perspective

"Why should we be in such desperate haste," said Thoreau, "and in such desperate enterprises?" Why do we let ourselves want so much and get so busy and burdened?

When will we learn that the trade we so often make of time and freedom for things, money, or excess involvement is a bad deal? And when will our society outgrow the rather juvenile notion that big and complex is better than small and simple?

"Besides the noble art of getting things done," said an Oriental philosopher named Lin Yü-t'ang, "there is the more noble art of leaving things undone." (And knowing which things are *not* worth doing, or having.) We admire the Gandhis of the world, who get rid of everything but their eyeglasses, scripture, and loincloth so that they can focus on what is important. We admire them, but we don't emulate them.

The ability to see things in clear perspective and the art

of simplifying can be gradually learned by developing the habit of asking ourselves three questions:

- Will it matter in five years? Or one year?
- What do I need more or less of in my life?
- How can I make this simpler?

Remember when your mother (or father or teacher) said, "If a thing is worth doing, it's worth doing well"? Well, it's not quite that black-or-white, especially not today. There are a few things worth doing well and there are an endless number of things not worth doing at all. But in between are *lots* of everyday things that need doing but don't need to be done perfectly. In fact they invite (and often reward) shortcuts and simplifying. "If a thing is just barely worth doing, just barely do it." Write *that* in the dust on your piano!

To know whether something is worth doing well, ask the three questions, "Will it matter in five years? Do I need it? Can I simplify it?" With the habit of these questions will come some new skills—the skill of discretionary neglect, the skill of selective prioritization, the skill of saying no, the skill of deciding what *not* to do, the skill of discerning which things are worth doing well, which things are just barely worth doing, and which things are not worth doing at all.

"Adding on" too often complicates our lives and contributes to the loss of self. "Casting off" simplifies our lives and helps us find ourselves.

Get into the habit of asking the three questions and categorizing things as to how you'll do them (*well, just barely,* and *not at all*).

Get rid of what you don't need (things and tasks)!

Acquire a few very fine things! One nice piece in an otherwise empty place is more attractive than a roomful of rubbish. Trade money for time whenever you can, and never do the opposite. If you can afford a housecleaner to give you a few extra hours during a week, get one.

Reduce your wants! Understand that there are two definitions of financial independence. One is having enough money to buy everything you want; the other is wanting less than what you are able to buy.

Simplify!
Simplify!

The Three Things That Matter

We took all of our children to Mexico one summer and spent six weeks in Ajijic, a little mountaintop fishing village high above Guadalajara. I (Linda) was in the midst of writing a book and needed background material and solitude, but the primary reason for our trip was to give the children perspective on the privileged lives they lead.

Because we had no car while we were there, we arranged for horseback transportation. A little Mexican man would arrive every third day with eight horses (the smallest two children rode double) and peso signs gleaming in his eyes at such a large account. (It cost approximately twelve dollars to rent eight horses for two hours.)

Each time we rode along the beach, we saw the village women pounding their washing on the rocks, and when we clip-clopped through the village streets, we saw families with ten children in one room. With eyes wide, our children gazed into the eyes of the native children, whose eyes showed reciprocal amazement.

One little nine-year-old Mexican girl visited our condo every day. Too shy to venture in at first, she became braver each day as she watched the children play in the small front-yard swimming pool. Neatly dressed in the same blue dress and no shoes, she was always smiling and happy and came day after day to interact with our children (who were not the least bit inhibited by the language barrier), but turned down all our invitations to go swimming with us. On the last Wednesday before we left, she finally consented to swim. We were all amazed when she jumped into the pool in her blue dress. At that moment we realized that she had no swimming suit or shoes—nothing besides the clothes she wore.

Our leftover food went to her family on the day we left. When we delivered it, we found a happy family in a home with only three walls, and a muddy front yard, occupied by a cow, a pig, and two chickens.

When we asked our own nine-year-old what she had learned from our time in Mexico, she said, "That you don't need shoes to be happy."

Unlike the problems of the people in Ajijic, Mexico, the problems of "fast track" Americans do not stem from scarcity or lack of options or challenges. Instead our challenge is whether we can sort out and choose and balance the most important and meaningful things from among all the needs and demands and options that surround us.

We once asked a seminar audience what needs or aspects of their lives they were trying to get in balance. It was like opening a dam. We were trying to make a list on the blackboard, but it was hard to write fast enough:

Career
Spouse
Sleep
PTA
Hobbies
Exercise—fitness
Lessons (piano, dancing, etc.)
Civic involvement
Television
Kids' soccer
Appearance (care of self)
Culture, music
Social and friends
Second jobs—extra money
Dentists, orthodontists, doctors
Voluntary work, service
Meditation, time to think
Charity and service to others
Children
Recreation
Church obligations
Social engagements
Reading for recreation
Travel
Reading to stay informed
the Internet
Talents (using them, developing them)
Solitude
Care of car and other possessions
Little League
Relatives (staying in touch)
Household maintenance and upkeep

Lawyers, accountants, and taxes
Poetry, art, and sensitivity to beauty
Loafing—doing nothing for a while
Shopping

Too many things! It's hard even to keep them all in mind—let alone find *time* and thought for each.

If we can reduce the things we are trying to balance to a small number, if we can categorize the important things into a few key areas, we can increase our chances of achieving balance.

The easiest number of areas to balance is *three*. It's relatively easy to juggle three balls, whereas four are many times more difficult. The mind can stay consistently conscious of three areas. With four or more, some are always overlooked or forgotten. A triangle has no opposite corners or side, each is connected to all. A three-legged stool is stable on any rough terrain.

Lifebalance is best pursued when we create three areas of priority. They are *family, work,* and *self.* The deepest and truest priorities of life all fit somewhere within these three categories.

Most people quickly accept family as one of the top three priorities. And work is such a necessity for most of us that it is no argument. Women who choose to stay home with small children have the challenging and important career of domestic management as the second of their three "balance points."

But many people question the third area. Should self be one of the three points on which we balance our day? Doesn't that imply a certain selfishness or self-centeredness? What about service to others? What about prayer or religious commitments? What about civic or community involvements or responsibilities?

If viewed correctly, the prioritizing of self does not eliminate these things, it *includes* them.

Often the best way to serve others is by taking care of ourselves and by changing ourselves for the better. (Ultimately this is the *only* way, because water cannot be drawn from a dry well.) We don't get to be better parents by changing our kids, or better friends by changing those around us. We become better parents and better friends and better able to serve others as we grow and develop within ourselves.

And just as we increase our ability to serve others by improving ourselves, so also we enhance ourselves by involving ourselves in service.

When we ask ourselves, "What do I need today?" the answer, at least part of the time, should have to do with service—"I need to fulfill my civic or religious assignment." "I need to help someone in need." "I need to be needed."

There is a necessity for balance *within* the third balance point of self. Some days we need something just for our outer or inner selves—such as a nap, some exercise, a little time to read, prayer or meditation. Remember that even very self-serving things can be done with others in mind—doing them will make you a better parent to your children, a better friend to your friends, a better member of the community. Other days our self-priority should be some kind of service, such as making a call to cheer someone up or doing a church assignment or working as a volunteer. Remember that this kind of thing, while aimed at others, is still an important factor in what you as a *self* are becoming.

With this clarification, most people are able to agree that

the three priorities of life that require daily thought (if life is to be balanced) are "family," "work" and "self." *The first step in obtaining Lifebalance is to spend five minutes each day, before you write down any other plans or think about your schedule, deciding on the single most important thing you can do that day for your family, for your work, and for yourself.* List these three choose-to-dos *before* listing any have-to-dos.

Even if you do nothing each day except the three key priority items, in a year you will have accomplished over three hundred specific, clearly thought out things for family, for self, and for work.

Remember that the key lies *not* in balancing our *time* equally between the three balance points (although each balance point does need some time each day) but in balancing our *thought*, our mental effort. And thinking hard enough to establish one single priority for each day will cause your mind to stay aware of all three areas all day long.

By narrowing down and naming the three balance points, we begin to gain control.

Having a Well-Managed Midlife Crisis . . . on Purpose

The much-talked-about, much-feared, much-experienced *midlife crisis* is sometimes triggered by an event (a divorce, a career disappointment, a health problem). Other times it just creeps up on us, escorted along by advancing age, declining physical condition, increasing stress, or the evaporation of the belief that we will ever be what we thought we would be.

The results of midlife crisis range from negative effects, such as silly and dangerous attempts to regain the look and feel of youth, to positive effects, such as getting into better shape or conducting a serious reassessment of what is important in your life.

Instead of waiting for a midlife crisis to strike, why not take the offense and stage a good early midlife crisis for yourself, on your own terms, with the objective of making some reassessment and some priority adjustments *before* some event forces you to do so?

The best way to start is to mentally divide your life into seasons. One of the most quoted verses in the Bible tells us, "To everything there is a season." Think of your youth, your education, the beginning or "planting" of your career, and of your family as the spring. Think of the full "blooming," family rearing, career-advancing middle portion of years as the summer. Think about the rich, late-career time as fall, when you may have the greatest opportunities to "harvest" your best ideas and biggest dreams. And think about the reflective, freedom-filled retirement years as the winter.

With these "seasons" as your framework, ask yourself what your priorities are for each phase of life. What are the things you will have unique access to and opportunities for in each season? Children ordinarily come only in late spring or early summer, and the raising of children is usually over by fall. Certain kinds of freedom (physical capacity, few things to tie us down) usually peak in the spring. Other kinds of freedom (financial, material) may arrive with the winter. Wisdom and perspective and the related abilities to give public and private service are not fully unfolded until fall.

Lay out your life like seasons. Decide what your priorities are in each. Ask yourself a lot of questions. Use your own knowledge of yourself and the suggestions in this book to find your own answers. This process, of segmenting, if it does nothing else, will make your life seem longer.

We said earlier that problems with balance result in part from having too many options—and too much freedom. The other side of the coin is that we are the first people in history who have enough alternatives and enough agency and choice to actually be able to design the kind of lives we want to live and the kind of people we want to be.

Doing so should be the reason for, the agenda of, and the objective behind the decision to have a midlife crisis on purpose.

Sunday Saw Sharpening

As a small boy (Richard), my favorite place was the university woodwork department, where my Gepetto-like Swedish grandfather taught. The airy shop had dozens of lathes, jigsaws, and other machines, all powered by the network of moving belts overhead. The room was always filled with the whine of the saws and the smell of sawdust. I was too young to operate the power tools, but I loved to watch—and Grandfather did let me build things with his wonderful Swedish hand tools.

One day he handed me a crosscut saw and a board. I tried to saw it in half, but the saw was so dull! I remember my right arm aching. I was sawing so furiously that smoke seemed to come from the board, but the cut lengthened very slowly. When I finally had to rest, with the board less than one-fourth sawed through, Grandfather took the file and in less than five minutes sharpened the saw. I reinserted it into my little cut, and *vroom, vroom,* a few quick pushes and the severed piece fell away. What power, what efficiency, what a feeling of purpose and effectiveness. So much less physical effort and so much more result.

I remember Grandfather telling me that one good sharpening kept the much-used saw sharp for a full week.

In our busy, stressed, competitive world, too many lives operate something like this:

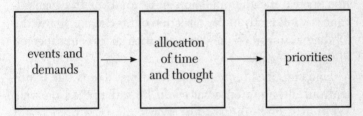

The demands on us and all the "things we have to do" control how we "spend" our time and thought. Over the years the things we spend our hours and our efforts on become our working priorities, whether we like it or not.

What we need is a way to reverse the arrows—to cause our true priorities to determine how we allocate our time and thought. Gradually this will modify and change the demands we make on ourselves, and even alter the events around us.

The sawing analogy is so apt. How common it is to feel as if we are working hard, busy all the time, tired all the time—yet not much is getting done.

Prioritizing and balanced goal setting *is* saw sharpening. A little time set aside to think about what matters and how to go about the things we want to be about can make all the difference. A good sharpening can keep us sharp all week.

Sunday is the ideal day to "sharpen." It is the first day of the week and the best time to think about the other six. If you think of Sunday as a day of *recreation,* adjust your definition a little so it will read *"re-creation"* of who you are and what you want to become. If you think of Sunday as a day of worship, remember that one way to praise God is to make something more of ourselves.

Think of Sunday Saw Sharpening as the organizing of dreams and the practical use of imagination. You will then find special meaning in Thoreau's promise: "If a man advances confidently in the direction of his dreams to live the life he has imagined, he will meet with success unexpected in common hours."

Thinking ahead, one week at a time, keeps our minds and our attention on what *could* be rather than on what Whittier called "the saddest words of voice or pen—'it might have been.' "

Set aside half an hour each Sunday to think, to reassess, to jot down goals and schedules for the week ahead. Focus your attention and your faith on the three corners of the triangle—on family, on work, on self. What can you do that is meaningful for each of the three during the week ahead? How can each of the three be balanced and work for rather than against the other two?

People who are worried about their ability to do this kind of regular prioritizing and balancing usually have two concerns: First, they don't have *time*; second, they don't know *how*. Neither excuse is valid. To say you don't have time to think and plan is like saying you don't have time to sharpen a saw. "Sharpening" is a time*saving* activity. It allows us to get much more done, and to do it better, with less hassle.

And this whole book is about *how*! Saw sharpening is an art and a skill that is learned by practice. Begin by setting aside a half hour each Sunday. If Sundays are busy, consider getting up a half hour earlier to have some thinking time before the start of the day. Saw sharpening is almost more restful and more renewing than the half hour of sleep it replaces.

Whatever time of day you start your Sunday session, don't begin by scheduling or thinking about all the things you "have to do." Instead, start by reminding yourself of the three balance point priorities and thinking about what you can do for and about each of them during the week ahead.

Living to Work or Working to Live

Ours is perhaps the only time in history where, instead of working to live, a vast number of people live to work.

Unfortunately living to work doesn't necessarily mean that we love our jobs. But our work is a major part of our identity. When we meet someone, the first question asked is, "What do you do?" For more and more of us, we *are* our jobs.

In other times and other societies work was thought of as the necessity—the means to other ends. People worked to feed themselves and to buy the time and means required to have access to more desired and more valued things, such as education; travel; leisure; the pursuit of music, art, poetry, history; or adventure.

So why has work become our preoccupation? Why, for so many, has work become the master and the manacle rather than the servant and the supplier?

Part of the reason may be that there are some very interesting and very pleasant jobs today. It's easy to understand why someone might get more excited about working twelve hours a day as a computer program designer, a space engineer, or an officer in an interesting and challenging company than his father got about his job as an assembly-line worker or a farm laborer.

But the real causes of our overorientation to work are the assumptions and expectations that we live with and the "norms" that surround us. Everyone works. People's identity is their work. It is very rare to ask questions such as "Do I really have to work?" "Do I really have to work *now* while I have preschool children at home?" "Do I really have to work as long as I do? As hard as I do?" "Is there work I would enjoy more even though I might not earn as much and even though the job might not sound as good to other people?" "If I didn't work quite as much, what else could I do with my time?" "Are there some ways we could simplify and thus need less money?" "Do I work more because it's easier than being at home?"

We don't ask these questions very often. Instead we're fond of saying, "I have to work." "We both have to work." "We simply require two incomes." "It just takes more and more to live every year." "I have to be more specialized all the time to stay on top." "I only have time for my own field of expertise."

Do some thinking—your *own* thinking. Instead of going along with what everyone else is doing, figure some things out for yourself.

In two-parent families it is not uncommon for 80 percent of the income of the second working parent to be used up in the extra costs of transportation, wardrobe, child care, and so forth. And this doesn't count the intangible costs paid by children who don't have the attention of either parent during the daytime hours. Of course both parents of many young children do have to work, as do most single parents, but the questions should at least be asked. And working and concentrating on small children does not always have to be "either-or." Options such as job sharing, part-time, flextime, and working at home are proliferating, and more and more men and women are finding creative ways to do both.

Whoever you are and whatever your job is, watch yourself so that you don't do too much trading of freedom and time for money and things. It is always a bad trade. Ask yourself if you really need the extra things, or newer things, or better things enough to give up more and more of the most valuable commodities, freedom and time.

Bertrand Russell's statement bears repeating: "It is the preoccupation with possession, more than anything else, that prevents men from living freely and nobly."

And Thoreau adds, "The true cost of a thing is the amount of what I call 'life' which is required to be exchanged for it immediately or in the long run."

Remember: There are two ways to be financially independent. One is to have unlimited money; the other is to have limited needs. Many of our things are not only unnecessary, they are worrisome and time-consuming and freedom-consuming.

Nationally-syndicated columnist Ellen Goodman put it this way:

What of we who suffer from mid-life bulge, the years of small children and big career plans, when it's hard to keep any sort of juggling act in place?

. . . There are times when we all end up completing a day

or a week or a month as though it were a task to be crossed off with a sigh. In the effort to make it all work, it can become all work. We become one-minute managers, mothers, husbands. We end up spending our time on the fly.

Marriage: Sharing and Synergy

Marriage can be anything from a casual liaison of mutual attraction or convenience to a magical combination that includes "oneness" $(1 + 1 = 1)$ as well as synergy $(1 + 1 = 3$ or more$)$. Most people who are married can take steps to build and enhance synergy. Most people who are not married are seeking someone with whom synergy can develop.

Synergy means a situation in which the total is greater than the sum of its parts. Sharing and communication combine with commitment as ingredients for synergy.

While *synergy* is usually a word used in business, its primary application ought to be in marriage. Two people who live together, who communicate and share, who know each other's strengths and weaknesses, who love each other partly because of their similarities and partly because of their differences . . . two such people have incredible opportunity for synergy.

In the first place they can decide who does what best and organize their life together around a degree of specialization where each partner plays the roles and does the tasks that he or she enjoys most and does best.

In the second place common, shared goals viewed from two separate perspectives make life a team sport rather than an individual effort. And everything from accomplishment to beauty intensifies and grows as it is shared.

Occasionally, in our seminars, we ask several couples to stand up and try to tell as accurately as they can what their spouse does during a normal day. We always find out how little most of us know about our spouse's life. The responses are usually very general: "Well, he goes to his office; he talks on the phone; he writes letters, I guess." "Aaahhh . . . well, she helps people decorate their houses—goes with them, I guess, and picks out things."

We know some couples who hold an "executive session" together each week—a short block of time on Sunday in which they work out their schedules for the week and decide who will do what.

Others try to take at least one short overnight trip together each month, even if it's just to a local motel, and to use the time to communicate, to reassess their goals, and to think about their own careers and futures as well as about the progress and development (and problems) of their children.

Synergy is produced in situations where two people support each other and consciously try to dovetail their abilities in working together. The support has to go both ways. Happily our society is getting away from the notion that the wife's only role is to support her husband or that a home is to support (or be at the mercy of) people's careers. A better perspective is that of mutual support and the notion that what happens *outside* the home supports what goes in *inside* the home. C. S. Lewis could have been speaking of the father *or* the mother when he said, "The homemaker has the ultimate career. All other careers exist to support this ultimate career." So however the "inner" career is shared or divided, the "outer" careers should be thought of as support rather than vice versa.

Many marriage partners *talk* a lot to each other but rarely *communicate*. Real communication needs to involve ideas, perspectives, and insights. People who only talk about other people are essentially gossiping. People who only talk about problems, or each other's faults, or why the checkbook won't balance, tend to lose respect for each other rather than gain it.

Reading together is one way of prompting communication about ideas. Balancing and scheduling time together is another way. The "five-facet review" discussed in the following section is still another. Hosting literary or discussion groups is another. Praying together is perhaps the best way of all.

Work at communicating more with your spouse about more things. Set aside time, schedule certain regular periods to talk, to work together, to brainstorm, to share. Use travel time and other routine moments together to plan and think collectively and to develop synergy.

Parenting by Objective

I (Richard) had spent the better part of the day at my management consulting office with a small business owner who was having some problems. My first question (as with almost every client) was, "What are your objectives for your business?"

This man didn't know. With a vague, rather blank look on his face, he said, "Well . . . let's see . . . to make a profit, I guess."

I was astounded by a man who had a business but didn't know what he wanted for it or from it. "You can never manage something effectively," I told the man, "until you have clear objectives."

That evening we had an unusually rough time with our three small children. Linda just happened to say, "Why are these children so hard to manage?"

What irony! I had spent the whole day telling a man he couldn't manage his business until he had clear objectives. What were our objectives with our children? I asked myself, and about the best answer I could produce was disturbingly similar to what I'd heard earlier that day, "Well . . . let's see . . . to *raise* them, I guess."

If specific objectives are so critical to our third or fourth priority (our work), then they must be critical to our first priority (our family).

That night was a real new beginning for us as parents. Linda and I began the process of defining our objectives for our children, a process that eventually led to the writing of five books: *Teaching Your Children Values* (an outline of twelve universal values, and methods for teaching them to children of all ages); *Teaching Your Children Joy* (a method for teaching preschool children twelve different forms of social, emotional, and physical joy); *Teaching Your Children Responsibility* (methods for teaching twelve forms of responsibility to elementary-age children); *Teaching Your Children Sensitivity* (techniques for helping adolescents to forget about themselves); and *Three Steps to a Strong Family* (setting up a family legal system, a family economy, and a set of value-building family traditions).*

We found that by having clear goals about what we

---

* All five books are published by Simon & Schuster (Fireside). Further help with parenting by objective is available through the Eyres' HOMEBASE program. Call (801) 581-0112.

wanted to teach our children at certain ages, and by focusing on *one* objective each month, we were able to *simplify* parenting and better measure or see just how effective we were at it.

Start off by forgetting the notion of "quality time" as a substitute for quantity time. It doesn't work. A parent who says "I don't have much time to spend with my kids, but the time I do spend is quality time" is usually kidding his kids as well as himself. It's as though the parent is saying to the children, "Okay, kids, I've got five minutes. We're going to have fun now whether you like it or not."

Usually it is a *quantity* of unhurried, unplanned time that generates *quality*. And there is sometimes a need simply to set aside some time just to be with children, whether you can afford the time or not.

The single most effective thing parents can do to improve the quality of the time they spend with their children is to have some idea of what they are trying to give or teach their children—to have, in other words, some clear and specific objectives.

Be careful as you set parenting objectives. Be sure you are setting goals for yourself in terms of what you want to give your children. Don't set goals for what you want your children to be. Too often parents decide they want a child to be a great artist or athlete or doctor or lawyer, without much reference to what the child wants or to what his or her gifts and attributes are. The notion of a child as a lump of clay that a parent can mold into whatever he or she wants is dangerous and damaging. A much better metaphor is that of a seedling, which, while it may be difficult to distinguish from other tiny trees when it is tiny, nonetheless possesses the potential to grow into a beautiful poplar or oak or sycamore or whatever it *is*. It will never grow into some other kind of tree. The efforts of the gardener-parent should not be to change its species but to *learn* (by observing) what kind of a tree it is and then to nourish it into the finest, healthiest, most productive tree of its particular kind.

We were living in London when our oldest son, Josh, turned five. He was, in my (Richard's) mind at least, a basketball star in embryo. I had commented on the size of his hands and the quickness of his reflexes before we got him out of the delivery room, and I had put a basketball in his crib long before he had ever seen a rattle. The fact that Josh never showed any interest at all in the sport had not deterred me.

But we were in England, where no one played basketball. The boy was deprived, and I, as his father-coach, was not going to stand for it. Eventually I heard about an exhibition game between two American service teams on the other side of London.

The problem was that when we got there, I couldn't get Josh to watch the game. He kept gazing around, mostly *up*. I said, "What are you looking at up there, son?" Josh looked at me, his eyes wide with excitement. "Those numbers up there, Dad. The ones on the outside keep going up by twos, and the one in the middle keeps going down by ones."

It was the scoreboard! The only way I finally got Josh to watch short parts of the game was by telling him that it was the ball going through the basket that made those two outside numbers go up.

What a lesson—for me. From then on I committed myself to looking at and into my children, to try to see what was really there, rather than looking for shadows of myself or extensions of my ego.

Generally speaking, schools have a stereotyping influence on our children. They *school* our children rather than *educate* them (*school* is here defined as "convergent learning," where everyone is supposed to come up with the "right answer," whereas *educate* is defined as "divergent learning," where creativity is valued above conformity and where a child's good questions receive more praise than his pat answers).

Schooling may be the responsibility of the state, but education is the responsibility of the parents.

Remember the goal of balance as you set objectives for what you want to give your children. Don't push small preschoolers into highly academic preschool situations before they are ready. They *can* learn to play the violin when they are two or to do square roots when they are three. But if they do these things at the expense of a real childhood or as an ego boost for parents who would like to brag about their "prodigy," then it is a deep and lasting mistake.

Books like ours, which give parents methods for teaching children various kinds of joys, responsibilities, and sensitivity, can be helpful in setting and reaching such goals for what you want to give your children. They can also help you with techniques for enhancing and developing your children's uniqueness. But there is something else that is much more valuable (and more personally and uniquely relevant) in the process of parenting by objective. We call it a *five-facet review*. It will help you to keep your child's life in balance and to arrive at objectives that are precisely right for your own particular and unique children. It works like this:

Once a month take your spouse (or if you are a single parent, take a close friend or relative who knows and loves your children) on a special "date." Go to a quiet restaurant together and limit your agenda to one topic—your children. Think about them one at a time by asking yourself five questions about each: (1) How is he doing physically? (2) How is he doing mentally? (3) How is he doing emotionally? (4) How is he doing socially? (5) How is he doing spiritually? Discuss each question and make some notes. Brainstorm about the child. Let one question lead to another. Some of the questions will need only brief answers: "Fine, no problem. Everything going well." But others will raise a red flag of danger or a green flag of opportunity, and you'll find yourself saying, "There is something we need to do something about or nip in the bud or work on." Or, "There is an aptitude or potential or a gift we need to help him develop."

Out of this five-facet review will emerge three or four specific goals for the month ahead—things you can focus on that will provide results you can notice.

This type of *parenting by objective* will not only help your children to do better, it will help *you* to feel better and more balanced. It will also remind you that your children are your first priority—deserving your finest efforts in every way. We all need these reminders in order continually to view our children not as irritations or impediments but as priorities, as chosen challenges, and even as privileges.

You Owe Yourself

The remarkable thing about doing the right things for yourself is that it is the most unselfish thing you can do. We all know that is true—when we stop to think about it. We can do so much more for others when we take care of ourselves. It is when our health is good, when we feel secure, when we are rested, when we are stimulated that we find the inclination and the insight necessary to help others.

There are two similar-sounding but drastically different questions we can ask ourselves. One, if repeated often enough, will produce within us jealousy, envy, insecurity, and perhaps bitterness and even narcissism. The other question, frequently asked, will lead to self-esteem, well-being, and to balance. The first, dangerous question is What do I want? The second, nourishing question is What do I need? The second question is not only a better one, it's a *tougher* one. Figuring out what you need takes more honesty, more courage, and more discernment than thinking about what you want. We have a friend who runs the creative department of a huge New York advertising agency and who is refreshingly candid about his field. "Advertising," he says, "is the subtle art of making people think they need what they actually only want."

The answer to the What do I need? question is often made easier and clearer by subdivision. Ask yourself, *What do I need physically?* (Exercise? Rest? Less food? More food?), *What do I need mentally?* (Stimulation? Meditation?), *What do I need emotionally?* (Solitude? Privacy? A little treat for myself?), *What do I need socially?* (Interaction? New acquaintances? A quiet chat with an old friend?), and *What do I need spiritually?* (Prayer? Chances to serve?)

Get in the habit of asking these questions weekly during your Sunday session, then following through on the answers during the week ahead.

One year, when our children were very young, I (Linda) became aware of how completely I was neglecting myself. I was caught up in the "martyr syndrome." It seemed that everything I was doing was for someone else, whether it was feeding husband and children, doing things for neighbors and friends, running errands hither and yon, assigning food for the PTA carnival, or preparing a Sunday school lesson. There was no time for myself or for my needs. After much frustration and contemplation I decided it was time to do something just for me.

Thinking back over the years, I realized that one of my happiest times was when I was playing in a string quartet with three friends. I knew it would be difficult, maybe even crazy, to revive the group, because all the members now were mothers with preschool children and babies at home.

To my delight, when I called them I found that the others were as anxious to get back into music as I was. With our common love for music, we prepared a concert over the next few weeks. We practiced with some children dancing in the background, some lying in our laps, some crying for peanut butter sandwiches, and a baby hanging on to the cello tailpin.

The concert was a triumph in many ways.

One of the most obvious applications of the concept of balance is taking a little time and thought for yourself each day. It can refresh you. It can revitalize you. It can sharpen your perspective. It can send you back to the tasks of the day with more vigor and less resentment. And it can make each day more varied and more pleasant.

Also, in a way that is not fully explicable, it can increase your self-esteem perhaps through the subtle suggestion that you are worth doing something for every day. As

Churchill said, "We are all worms, but I have decided that I am a glowworm."

Finally, as was said earlier, there is a predictable but seldom-discussed connection between doing good things for ourselves and doing good things for others. After asking *What do I need?* and filling that need, it is easier and more natural to ask, *What do others need? What can I give?*

Service, particularly anonymous service, can be exciting as well as fulfilling, and we seem more inclined toward it when we are taking good care of ourselves.

Do it! Form the habit of asking yourself what you need every day. Then do something about it.

Whom Do You Admire?

Admiration is an interesting quality. It can cause envy, jealousy, and discontent, or it can motivate and stimulate people to become more than what they are.

"Beware of what you want," it has been said, "for you will get it." Paraphrased, the saying could also read, "Beware of whom you admire, for you will grow to be more like them."

Whom do you admire? Whom do you envy? It's an interesting question, because in its answer we can learn a considerable amount about ourselves.

Answers to this question, on a general level, are fairly predictable. In fact they can be categorized into a fairly small number of groups. Many admire wealth, because they believe it brings freedom and enjoyment. Many admire power. Many admire fame. Professional athletes are often envied, as are acclaimed artists and performers, and corporate presidents and successful politicians.

It occurred to us not long ago that we had personal friendships with a few people in these admired categories. And it occurred to us that it would be interesting to know whom *they* admire. Do they admire themselves? Do they admire one another? Or are they so self-satisfied that they envy no one?

Well, we asked four of them—the chief executive of a major corporation, a venture capitalist who has accumulated major wealth, an international sports star, and a nationally known television personality.

The results were somewhat surprising, or maybe they weren't so surprising after all. *They all admired balance.* They each had their own way of stating it, but all of them essentially said they admired people who found time for the important things in life—for family, for relationships, for growing inwardly and developing their talents. Because of their own achievements and visibility, they saw the relative unimportance of wealth, power, and fame and found it a little amusing that other people would admire and envy them for those things.

Balance is what the admired admire.

It is as though we all have, without consciously realizing it, different levels of success in our minds. Someone who achieves wealth or position, recognition or power, is successful on one level. But someone who is secure within, who enjoys the love and respect of his or her family, and who manages to pretty well *balance* his or her life—such a person is successful by a higher (and deeper and more "inner") definition of the word.

One wealthy business leader, president of a major U.S. corporation, defined success as "noseprints on the window." What he meant was that you are a success if your children wait with anticipation for you to come home each night. He was in agreement with Mencius, who said, "A great man is one who does not lose his child's heart."

Inner feelings are a far better measure of success than outer appearances; we are far more capable of evaluating our own success than that of others.

Discover and enjoy balance in your life between work, family, and self. And while you may still notice those with more things or higher public profiles, you will have the assurance that you have something too valuable to trade for any of it.

Implementing Priority Balance

"WORKING THE TRIANGLE" AND "SHARPENING THE SAW"

Making a Change in Habits

Even if you agree with most of the observations and ideas we have made about priority balance—even if you agree basically with *all* of them—there is no guarantee that they will have much impact on how you live or on how you balance your own life.

Change is difficult, especially changing *basic* things, such as how we use our time and how we "spend" our conscious thought.

Ideas are fun, and most of us enjoy reading things and thinking to ourselves, *Right on! This is just what I need,* or *These people are saying just what I've been thinking.* But the stimulation provided by ideas or accepted suggestions is not usually the same stimulation required for implementation and real change.

Change rarely comes naturally. Even if there's no debate at all about whether we should change. Implementation takes work—mental work, which can change the *habits* of our minds and of our actions.

We said earlier that most unbalance is the result of bad habits. We get rid of bad habits most effectively when we replace them with new, good habits. The priority-balance concepts and conclusions discussed so far can be *manifested* and *implemented* through two new, simple, good habits.

(The problem with these two habits is they are so basic and straightforward that they may seem *too* simple. But theirs is the simplicity of grace and efficiency, not of naïveté or inexperience. Benjamin Disraeli said, "I would not give a fig for the simplicity that lies this side of complexity, but I would give my right arm for that which lies beyond.")

The first habit (a daily one) is "working the triangle."

Consider what was mentioned earlier—the unique strength of a triangle's shape:

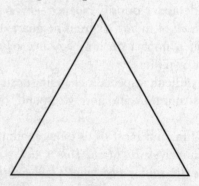

Three corners, each connected to the other two. No opposites. You can't crush it or skew it because each side holds the other two in place. There is stability because each corner finds its level independent of the other two and yet supports the other two. (As noted before, a three-legged stool is solid on uneven ground.)

Now let's label the three corners with our three priorities, or "balance points," that we've discussed:

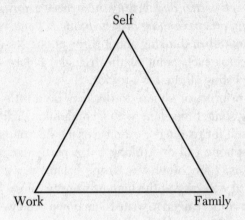

Self

Work   Family

Each of the three corners balances the other two . . . and
supports the other two . . . and draws from the other two.
Think about the connections for a minute. The way we
build and develop (and enjoy) ourselves is through our
work and through our families. We try to teach families
the work and skills of achievement and the respect of self
and individuality. And our work and careers are *for* our
families and the fulfillment of self and contributions to
others.

The danger lies not so much in forgetting that all three
are important but in letting other, less important things get
ahead of them or in allowing them to get out of balance
with each other.

Balancing needs to occur daily. If we think about it once
a year or once a month, or even once a week, we will look
back and find we've been tipping—tilting away from balance a little each day so that we can't get level again.

Daily balancing is accomplished by the habit of working the triangle every day—by setting one single priority each day for each corner and writing these three priorities down before any other planning or scheduling is done.

It's a matter of thinking about three choose-to-dos each day (one for each point of the triangle) *before* thinking about or listing all the have-to-dos.

Each priority, or choose-to-do, may be a little thing—spending some time alone with a child, taking a little time for yourself for reading or exercise or meditation, making a difficult phone call or working out a particular problem.

There isn't any other way. To be balanced, we need to think until we arrive at the highest priority for each corner each day. And we need to write them down. And we need to do them.

Doing so may change just a little how we spend our time and how we live the day. But it also changes our habits of thinking. It trains our minds to consider and be aware of all three corners or balance points every day.

Whatever planner or schedule or list you use, whether it's an elaborate time-management Day-Timer or a plain sheet of paper, start out by making three short "priority blanks" at the top of each day for "Self," for "Family," and for "Work." Fill them each in with a *need*—with a small thing you didn't have to do but that you decided to choose to do. The family need might be as simple as asking about the book Terry's reading for English or calling a cousin with whom you've been out of touch. The personal need might be to exercise or to take a short, quiet walk. The work need will usually involve a person who could use appreciation or a compliment you decide to give.

Think of each blank as one corner of the balanced triangle. Ponder each long enough to come up with the day's three balanced priorities with three choose-to-dos that you list *before* getting into the scheduling of the have-to-dos. This kind of mental work is hard, but it is not unpleasant. The five minutes you spend thinking about it will become the most refreshing, most satisfying part of your day.

And the habit of *working the triangle* will become the key to your personal Lifebalance!

There is a second habit, this time a weekly one, that can make working the triangle more effective. Spend a half hour each Sunday "sharpening your saw," or thinking about what you want to do during the week ahead. Use the three balance points of the triangle as your model in these Sunday sessions. Think in terms of what you want to do during the coming week in the three areas of family, self, and work. Write the goals down and use them as reference points each day when you work your triangle.

The weekly saw-sharpening Sunday session becomes a time to ponder the relative importance of family, work, and personal needs. It can also be an organized, productive time to refine longer-range goals, to divide your life into balanced "seasons," and to have the intentional, productive, and ongoing midlife crisis mentioned earlier.

The good daily habit of *working the triangle* and the good weekly habit of *saw sharpening* have the power to break down the various bad habits of unbalance. As you develop these two habits, you will be participating and implementing each of the priority balance principles in this first section—simplifying and perspective, focusing on the things that matter, conducting an ongoing "midlife crisis," subordinating work to life, developing synergy, parenting by objective, caring for yourself, and finding balance.

Attitude Balance

BALANCING STRUCTURE WITH SPONTANEITY

Attitudes

What are you?
Flesh? Bones? Mind? Personality?
Who are you?
Name? Job? Title?
Where are you?
Location? Progress?
Can one simpler, deeper answer
satisfy all three questions?

Our *attitudes*
Are what and who and where we are.
Attitudes aim our approach
To opportunities, to needs, to life,
But most of all they determine
Who we are within ourselves
And arbitrate the competition for dominance
Between structure and spontaneity,
Between firmness and flexibility,
Between the motor and the sail,
Between the left and right halves of our brain.

The second type of balance is *attitude balance*.

It is one thing to keep our priorities and responsibilities—the things we *do*—in balance with each other. It is another thing altogether to balance our actual selves—to create within ourselves the qualities of both discipline *and* flexibility, both structure *and* spontaneity; to develop an attitude that accommodates both the attitude of nose-to-the-grindstone work and the kind of free, footloose fun that activates the intuitive in-tune insights of the right hemisphere of the brain and balances it with the logical mathematical left.

The society we live in seems to want us to choose between the two—to typecast ourselves as either firm or flexible, either fastidious or fun, either serious or silly, either button-down professional or blue-jeaned ski bum.

Yet within ourselves we know that to keep our sanity in an ever-crazier world, we need at least a little, and hopefully quite a bit, of *both* sides, both attitudes.

The observations of this section are designed not only to convince you that both attitudes are possible but also to strongly suggest that, with balance, they are complementary rather than competitive.

Jets and Hot-Air Balloons

Is the objective to get there or is it to enjoy the journey?

Why do we get on jets? The answer is obvious—to get somewhere as quickly and efficiently as possible.

Why do we get in hot-air balloons? Some may say, "Well, I don't—and I won't." (Remember you said that, because it's part of the point.) Those who get in a hot-air balloon

certainly do not do so to get somewhere. The only predictable thing about hot-air balloons is their unpredictability.
You don't know where you will go or when you will get
there. It all depends on the wind.

So why do people ride balloons? *To enjoy the journey!*

Is there room in life for both jet planes and hot-air
balloons . . . for both getting there and enjoying the journey?

Jet planes and hot-air balloons are not the only compari-
son that illustrates the difference. We can set up a whole
list:

GET THERE		ENJOY THE JOURNEY
swim upstream	vs.	flow with the current
left-brain logic	vs.	right-brain intuition
science	vs.	art
structure	vs.	spontaneity
discipline	vs.	flexibility
snowmobiles	vs.	cross-country skiing
outer	vs.	inner
yang	vs.	yin
motor boats	vs.	sailboats
planning	vs.	serendipity
set plays	vs.	freelance
acting	vs.	reacting

Most of us feel drawn to both sides of the list. We are
made up of both the yin and the yang. We contain both the
sensitivity of sails and the momentum of motors. We all
want to get there *and* enjoy the journey. And we know,
when we think about it, that neither goal can satisfy us for
very long without the other.

So often the reason people want to "get there" is that they believe getting there will help them to be successful or, in other words, happy. But it doesn't work that way, and people who do get there often find themselves saying something like "Is that all there is?" or, more philosophically, "I wish I had realized that happiness is in the journey, not in the destination."

If the journey is thought of only as the means to the end, it is rarely enjoyed, rarely appreciated. In fact it is begrudged. We resent the journey as well as the time it takes us to get to whatever we think the destination is. So we don't notice beauty, or opportunity, or needs along the way.

Poets and songwriters as well as philosophers keep reminding us to live in the present, to stop to smell the roses, to appreciate our children while they're young, and to be aware of the joys of the moment. But peer pressure, advertising, and our own ambition keep nagging us to *get there*.

The instinct to get there is so strong in some of us that even our vacations and our leisure lack the element of enjoying the journey. We plan every minute and worry if we're not at each new spot when our schedule says we should be or when we think we need to be.

I (Richard) took our young son on a hike one rare day. I knew it was important for us to be together, and our son was excited. There was a plateau we would climb to so that we would have a level place to camp.

The first part of the hike was great. We talked. We enjoyed being together. But we weren't moving very fast. I got a little upset at our slow pace and started pushing our son to walk faster. I finally found myself carrying his pack and almost dragging him.

We made it to the plateau just in time to set up camp

before dark. The boy fell asleep before I had the campfire going. When the flames grew and lit his face, I saw tear-stains.

There are always two goals. One is to get there. The other is to enjoy the journey. Too much emphasis on one can ruin the other.

We have a friend who has had some of the greatest (and most adventurous) vacations imaginable with his family. They make a point of planning nothing and of concentrating entirely on the surprises of each new moment. They just get in the car and "go west" or "go east"—watching and waiting to see what each day will hold.

I (Linda) sat in the Atlanta airport between flights one afternoon and watched parents interacting with their children. The "movie" that surrounded me could have been titled "Children Are a Useless Nuisance." One parent after another went by, tugging on crying children, saying "Don't touch that" in an irritated voice or yelling "You come back here this minute!"

Everyone was supposedly on the way to an exciting adventure (at least as far as the children were concerned)—to ride on a big airplane, or to meet Grandpa and Grandma—but the parents didn't seem to notice. They seemed irritated by the very presence of their children.

A couple of days later it was our youngest son, Eli's, third birthday, and I found myself alone for a few minutes in the kitchen while he was visiting at Grandma's. The older children were downstairs preparing a surprise birthday party for him. I was thinking how nice it would be in a few years when the children would be older and able to take care of themselves and the house would be this quiet all the time.

A few minutes later Eli arrived home. As the children

popped out from their hiding places to shout "Surprise!" and I heard the shrieks of delight and Eli's funny "Yahoo!" as he opened each present, I realized how silly it is not to savor every day with a child who would so quickly slip through our fingers and be off on his own.

How difficult it is to appreciate the present and enjoy the journey rather than wish for the past or the future! Even through the hassles and seemingly boring routines of life, it is crucial to remember that memories are being made *today*!

People can be categorized to a rather amazing extent by the first thing they think about when they wake up in the morning. There are the high-achievers, who bounce out of bed and say, *What can I accomplish today?* There are less positive but still very dutiful types, who say, *What do I have to do today?* And there are the burdened, defensive people, who essentially say, *I wonder what will happen to me today?*

But there may be a fourth alternative—a better thing to think with our first consciousness of the day. It is *What can I enjoy today? What are the challenges of this day? The responsibilities? The opportunities? And how can I enjoy them?*

The need of course is for balance. Someone who thinks only of *getting there* is more and more an insensitive, self-driven robot, while someone who thinks only of *enjoying the journey* can become an aimless, unfulfilled drifter.

The challenge is to remember that in everything, big and small, from a career to a vacation, from building a house to climbing a mountain, there are always two goals—to get there and to enjoy the journey. When we are conscious of both, it is usually possible to do both. And when both are not possible, we need to stop and think about which of the two goals is most important for that moment.

Antiplanning

What we have today is the classic example of the tarnishing of a good name. In the name of planning we have an incredible proliferation of time-management tools, executive Day-Timers, calendar and time-organizer programs for laptops, and exotic schedulers and organizing books filled with multicolored tabs and charts for everything.

The theory behind these planners of course is that they will help us get organized, help us be more efficient, help us get more done. And they do!

So why is it that the users and practitioners of highly detailed planning and time-management tools often seem to feel even more stress and frustration than nonusers?

Because getting more done is not the answer. Deep down most of us want more *quality*, not *quantity*. Balance is the answer. And most "planners" often have a negative effect on balance. Consider the following:

• Ninety-five percent of what is written in planners has to do with work, career, and money, so they are disproportionate and often destructive of the priority balance that should exist between work, family, and personal needs.

• Planners cause us to live by lists, to act rather than respond. If we're not careful, our lists control us rather than the other way around. (Have you ever done something that was not on your list and felt compelled to write it on your list and cross it off?) We begin to view things that are not on our lists as irritations and distractions rather than as opportunities, and we begin to lose the critical balance between structure and spontaneity.

• Because they are accomplishment-oriented, most planners focus our attention on things, on getting, and on *doing*, sometimes at the expense of people and giving and *thinking*. Thus they can be destructive to balance between achievements and relationships.

Lifebalance could be called *antiplanning* because it leads people in an opposite direction—toward more emphasis on family, spontaneity, and relationships.

Balance and quality of life are not so much a matter of getting more done as they are a matter of deciding what is important and spending time and thought on things that are meaningful, whether they are planned or not.

In the small Idaho town where we spend part of our summers, some farmers still plow their fields with horse-drawn plows. The horses are fitted with blinders so that they will keep their eyes (and their attention) on the furrow they are plowing rather than on the landscape or the sunrise or the female horse in the next pasture.

Highly structured planners and rigid to-do lists are a great deal like blinders. They give us tunnel vision and focus us so tightly on our schedule that we don't notice the beauty, or the opportunities, or the people and the needs that are around us.

Antiplanning means throwing away the blinders of rigid structure and planned inflexibility along with the big, bulky, overly-structured time organizers and day planners. It means realizing that the unplanned, even unexpected things in life are often more fulfilling than the calculated. It means enjoying rather than resenting the unexpected. It means setting goals (and even making lists), but remembering that the lists can be changed (or thrown out) if something more important or more beautiful comes along.

The term *antiplanning* also reminds us that setting goals and objectives is a very different kind of activity than planning and scheduling. Goals are the beacons and destinations that guide and energize our lives, and they should be clung to and committed to. Plans are for our best efforts (at the moment) to figure out how and by what course we will get to our goals. The goal is not dependent on the plan. If we are alert and if we cast off our blinders, we will find better ways and straighter courses to our goals. One way to say it is "Be strong in your goals and flexible in your plans."

Most of all, antiplanning means a different kind of thinking, which never allows work to supersede family or inner needs, which keeps *people* above *things,* and which spices the structure of our lives with frequent pinches of spontaneity.

Freeing the Mind

Some people plan because they love details. Others plan because they hate details and want to get them out of their minds by putting them on paper—they want to free their minds so that they can be receptive to beauty, to opportunity, and to ideas.

When do ideas come? Not when we're rushing, hurrying, worrying, scurrying; but on a beach, in the shower, driving, jogging, lying in bed, listening to a symphony.

The details of the day are dampeners and detractors to

ideas. It is as though the mind has a certain number of circuits, and when most of them are tied up with schedules and situations, details and dates, few are left free for creativity, for ideas, for spontaneity.

Sometimes the mind is freed by routine or simple activity. Shaving or showering uses only a few circuits, and since we're getting something done, our mind does not pressure us as much to think or worry, so most circuits are free. If we're sunbathing, we're getting tan; if we're jogging, we're getting in shape; if we're driving or flying, we're getting closer to our destination—so our "achievement trigger" can shut down, the "don't just sit there, do something" syndrome can deactivate, and we can be more aware, freer, more open to ideas and insights.

Another way of freeing the mind is with a pen. Quiet the noisy mind by writing down the clutter, deciding which things you do when, and then forgetting about them until their time comes. Clearing the circuits is the best reason for list making. Too many worrisome details occupying the mind not only block creativity, they screen and darken awareness and appreciation and the ability to feel.

Waimea Falls Park, on the windward side of Oahu in Hawaii, is one of the most breathtakingly beautiful spots on earth. Peacocks strut in lush, flowered meadows beneath massive banyan trees and below the cascading waterfall. We sat one day near the path, leaning back against the trunks of purple-flowering trees, and watched tourists go by, listened to their conversation, watched their faces, watched their eyes, tried to read their thoughts. All were saying (or thinking), "This is beautiful," but for some it was a small and quick passing thought, overshadowed by "bigger" notions such as:

How far is the waterfall; will I have time to get there and stay on schedule?

What should I take a picture of?

I wish the weather would brighten up; this would be prettier with sunshine.

Where are those kids? I wish they wouldn't wander off.

I'd better find a tour guide so that I'll know what to look at here.

I should have stayed with that jogging; I'm not in good enough shape to enjoy this hike.

I wish Hilda would walk faster; she's always walking behind me.

I haven't called the office in two days.

I know there is something I forgot to do before I left home.

Awareness of the present is the source of joy. Awareness is clouded by the same demanding, distracting details that clutter our minds and tie up our circuits. Free mental circuitry is the beckoner of beauty as well as the invitation to intuition and ideas. Mentally get rid of all the little pressing have-to-dos by writing them down. Carry a simple date book or schedule of some kind (altered by the three choose-to-do priority blanks discussed in the last section). Use it as storage for everything *except* awareness of the moment.

Serendipity

Horace Walpole, an eighteenth-century English writer, enjoyed reading Persian fables. One day he read one called "The Three Princes of Serendip"* (the ancient name for

---

* A full translation of this fable can be found in Richard Eyre's book *Spiritual Serendipity*.

the island of Ceylon, or Sri Lanka). It told of three young princes who went into the world to seek their fortunes. None found fortune, but each found something even better, things such as love, beauty, friendship, and peace.

Walpole was impressed by the notion of finding something other than (and better than) what was being sought. He felt a need for a word that could describe such "happy accidents" and (being a writer with the license to coin new words) came up with *serendipity*. The full definition he gave to the word was "that quality which, through good fortune and sagacity, allows a person to discover something good while seeking something else."

Walpole would not like the changed and simplified meaning that today's dictionaries give to his word. When we say serendipity is "a happy accident," we miss Walpole's main point. To him serendipity was something that could happen only if a person was aware and sagacious and only if he or she was seeking something else that gave him or her a basis on which to judge something else as better.

Think about the implications of the real definition. Serendipity is a *quality* that people can develop. It requires *sagacity* (awareness, understanding, wise observation, alertness), and it requires that we be *seeking something* (have goals, aims, objectives). The definition suggests that as we combine our sagacity with our structure, we will *cause* the phenomenon of discovering things that are better than what we are pursuing.

There was a period during my (Richard's) college years when I became obsessed with positive thinking and aggressive goal achievement. I felt that the world was at my feet, that I could do anything if I had clear enough goals and plans.

I was totally preoccupied with accomplishing and not the least bit worried whether what I wanted required the manipulation of other people. I don't remember any other time I felt so much in control (or any time I offended more people).

My bubble was burst by a girl I was dating who, in breaking off our relationship, said she was sick of my goals and plans and would rather be with someone more spontaneous and fun. She also called me many names, among which "selfish," "insensitive," and "manipulative" were the nicest.

By sheer coincidence our last date was to a concert by a group called the Serendipity Singers. The next day, still dazed and reeling from the previous evening's criticism, I found myself wandering around the library and, for want of anything better to do, looking up the meaning of the strange word the band used for a name. The dictionary's definition of *serendipity* fascinated me: "The quality of being aware and sensitive enough that you can find something good while looking for something else."

What struck me was that with an attitude of serendipity perhaps I could have goals and be looking for something and still be aware and sensitive enough to find good things I hadn't sought, and relaxed enough to be spontaneous. I could thus view the unexpected as opportunities rather than interruptions. I could be firm *and* flexible. I didn't have to choose between being an aggressive accomplisher and a sensitive ski bum.

I adopted *serendipity* as my favorite word and began to think of it as my personal need and my personal goal.

Years later, when our first child was born, I still thought so much of the word that we named her Saren. There aren't many kids who are named after a word! Actually I wanted to name her Serendipity, but Linda worried that the kids would call her "Dippy." When we had our first son, I wanted to name him after the English author who coined the word. Linda said that she understood my sentiment and that she would have gone along with me if only the author's name hadn't been Horace.

How can anyone be so in love with a word? Simply because its meaning can become a passage or a bridge between regions that are otherwise hostile to each other— lands that, without the "serendipity bridge," we have to choose between because the gap separating them is so wide.

One is the land of structure and discipline, of goal setting, positive mental attitude, and achievement. It seems to be inhabited mostly by high-powered business executives, aspiring upwardly-mobile type-A personalities, logical left-brain thinkers, and do-it-all superparents. The other is the land of spontaneity and flexibility, of sensitivity and observation and relationships. Here we find many artists, creative thinkers, philosophers, would-be Renaissance men or women, and people who use the intuitive right hemisphere of their brain.

Metaphorically the people in one land are more interested in *getting there,* so they travel in jet planes, power yachts, and snowmobiles. In the other land the main interest is in enjoying the journey, so people prefer hot-air balloons, sailboats, and cross-country skis.

Although there are overlaps, we generally associate people in each land with certain things: In the first land people read the *Wall Street Journal;* they dress for success, use big Day-Timers, and listen to motivational tapes. In the second land people read poetry, dress for comfort, watch sunsets, and listen to Stravinsky. In Land A politics means power, progress, military strength, and tax loopholes. In Land B politics means environmental conservation, peace marches, and compassion. In one land people live to work and say things such as "Act, don't react," and "Don't just sit there, do something." In the other land people work to live and say things such as "Go with the flow" and "Don't just do something, sit there."

The problem most of us have is that we like both lands . . . and we like lots of people in both lands. And there are certain parts of us that we know belong in each land. We realize that each of the two has its own unique beauty and usefulness. We know that we appreciate one all the more after we have spent time in the other—like going from the snow in Colorado to a beach in California.

It is serendipity that allows us to move freely back and forth . . . even to have a home in each land.

Remember that serendipity requires sensitivity and highly tuned observations so that we don't miss things such as beauty, needs, opportunities, ideas, and spontaneous moments. If we have this sensitivity and we have clear goals and objectives (because serendipity only "finds something good while looking for something else"), then we have both the passport and the visa that let us spend all the time we want in both lands.

With serendipity we can live comfortably in one land because we are "seeking things"—we have goals, we want to achieve, to grow, to progress. But we can also feel at home in the other land because we have awareness and sagacity and are therefore flexible and spontaneous enough to change our minds and change our course when the right moment or the right need or the right surprise comes into view.

People who have cultivated the bridge or the passport of serendipity can find real fulfillment in meeting a goal, in checking things off their to-do list, in competing and in winning. But they can also feel the joy in watching an approaching storm or in doing a spur-of-the-moment anonymous good turn, or in writing a poem, or in winning a small smile from a small child.

Serendipity is a bridge that lets us have our cake and eat it, too. We don't have to choose between being structured schedulers and flexible freelancers. We can have both goals and surprises, both plans and spontaneity, both discipline and flexibility. We can ride in jet planes and in hot-air balloons.

Serendipity is not luck, and it is not (despite its common brief definition of a "happy accident") accidental. Serendipity is *obtainable*. It is a quality that grows in people who develop their awareness and sensitivity and their commitment to flexibility *along with* their ability to set goals and plan their time.

"Act, don't react," we are told at positive-thinking rallies and by "success" books. Never be surprised. Be in charge, take control, decide what you want, and don't let anything get in your way.

What foolishness!

What an arrogant assumption to believe that we have total control over our own lives, that there will be no surprises, and that we can manage and manipulate all the things and all the people around us. And what a boring, unexciting prospect even if it could be true.

All we have hope of controlling is ourselves, and even

that is a pretty tall order. With concentration and effort we can control what we want, what we pursue, how we live, and how we respond to the people and the world around us.

Well-lived lives achieve balance and develop serendipity as a bridge between acting and reacting, between controlling and responding.

A well-balanced day includes not only things you did because you had planned to do them but unplanned things you did because you noticed them and chose to do them. For example:

- A mother, looking out of her office window, notices that it is an exceptionally beautiful afternoon and decides she could finish the work she is doing now early the next morning. She goes home early and takes her three-year-old to the zoo.

- A businessman reads an article that gives him an idea. He changes his schedule and makes some phone calls that end up providing him with a lucrative new client.

- A parent notices that her third-grade son looks troubled and puffy-eyed as he comes in from school. She asks if anything is wrong, and he bursts into tears. She decides she can get along for another day without grocery shopping and spends the next hour learning some very interesting things about some insecurities her son feels at school.

- A commuter, stuck in an impossible freeway traffic jam, exits off into a field, listens to music, watches the clouds and the sunset, and unexpectedly feels some clarity and some ideas regarding a problem he has been worrying about.

- A husband notices during dinner that his wife seems distracted, irritable, and cross with her children. He realizes it has been a while since they've been out together, so he forgets about the big game he'd planned to watch on TV, calls a baby-sitter himself, and takes his wife to a movie.

• A woman hosting a social gathering at her home hears the doorbell ring. Answering it, she finds an awkward, semiretarded boy, who slowly tries to explain to her that he is selling magazine subscriptions. The woman, who is not interested in the magazines and anxious to return to her party, nonetheless notices that the boy wears only a threadbare, thin coat on this chilly night. She gets the coat her son outgrew last year and gives it to the boy.

• A couple taking a weekend away for a sort of second honeymoon is waiting in a line at an airport to get a rental car. They strike up a conversation with a woman in the line, who happens to tell them of a marvelous, quaint little hotel. They change their original reservations and end up discovering a perfect place.

• A mother has set a goal to clean out her refrigerator, but just as she is starting, she notices that her two-year-old, for the first time she can recall, is looking at picture books of his own accord. She puts off the refrigerator for a while and reads to the child.

It is said that the archer hits the target partly by pulling, partly by letting go. Life needs to be lived partly by acting, partly by reacting; partly by initiating, partly by responding. It is as important to be sensitive to the needs of a child or to respond to a touching or beautiful moment as it is to accomplish a task or to make a decision.

Reacting, responding, deviating from your plan to tend to something that just came up are not signs of weakness. Nor are doubts and questions; nor is a strong interest in people other than yourself and in fields of expertise other than your own.

In some ways my (Richard's) years spent earning an M.B.A. from the Harvard Business School were among the most exciting and interesting of my life. I enjoyed the stimulation and thrived on the competition.

About halfway through the first year, however, I learned something about myself. I found myself feeling compelled to go "across the river" to the other parts of Harvard every once in a while, and felt like I needed to rub shoulders with liberal arts and philosophy or history majors. I needed contact with people who were trying to understand the world, not control it. I needed interaction with people who asked questions instead of giving answers and still had doubts once in a while, even about themselves. I needed to mingle with individuals who carried paintbrushes or telescopes instead of attaché cases, and who wore jeans or lab smocks instead of button-down collars and blazers.

The problem with so many of my business-school colleagues was that they were so bent on planning, on organizing, on solving, and on winning that they limited their world to what they could control and understand (which, by definition, leaves out the most interesting parts).

Serendipity is a remarkable quality—a bridge between lands that are otherwise unconnected. Perhaps the most amazing thing about serendipity is that it is so available. People who understand what it is and who consciously want it . . . find that they suddenly begin to have it.

Awareness, Superawareness, and Gratitude

Balance is largely dependent on awareness. Awareness, or sagacity, as Walpole called it, is what triggers serendipity and reveals to us the unplanned needs or opportunities for which we should be willing to depart from our routine or our plans.

It is our awareness of the current individual situations of family members and of our own personal needs that keeps us working at balancing the triangle; and it is awareness of beauty and feelings and setting and moods that makes life interesting and joyful. Thoreau wrote, "Only that day dawns to which we are awake." Writer and philosopher Wilfred A. Peterson tried to list the qualities of awareness. In addition to alert senses, he cited the following:

- Identifying yourself with the hopes, dreams, fears, and longings of others so that you may understand and help them
- Learning to interpret the thoughts, feelings, and needs of others through their words, tones, inflections, facial expressions, and movement
- Searching for beauty everywhere
- Knowing wonder, awe, and humility
- Discovering the mystic power of silence and coming to know the secret inner voice of intuition

Awareness expands our universe, expands our capacity, expands our abilities and our powers. Some have even said that the difference between man and God is a vast difference of awareness.

The mistake we make is in not thinking more about awareness. The more aware we are of awareness, the more of it we will have. The mind, in this instance, is an obedient subject. Tell it to notice more, and it will do so. We *develop* awareness by conscious effort. And the very things we want to result from our awareness are the things that help us to develop it.

In other words, cause and effect can be interchanged. Just as it is true to say, "The more aware we are, the better we will do at working the triangle and at having seren-dipity," it is also true to say, "The more we work at balancing the triangle and having serendipity, the more aware we will become." Deciding every day on a priority for family, work, and self inevitably makes us more aware of ourselves and of the people, needs, and situations around us. And the seek-ing of serendipity requires us to intensify our awareness.

I (Linda) remember one particular period of my life when I was struggling to lighten up a little. The stress of work and other commitments seemed so intense, I felt as if I was in a pinball game, bouncing from one task to another without looking up or looking around.

One day, while sitting at the hairdresser, I happened to read a short article on (of all things) the virtues of writing poetry. "All poems start with an observation," the article said. "Committing yourself to attempt a small poem on a regular basis will require you to *observe* and then to *think*. And these are the two things that awareness is made of."

I tried it and it worked. The type of thinking that it took to attempt a poem lifted me above the day's routine and brought about, at least for the moments involved, a new level of awareness.

In his remarkable book *A Guide for the Perplexed,*

E. F. Schumacher divides the things that occupy this planet into four "levels of being": (1) mineral (M, or matter without life); (2) plant (M + L, or matter with life); (3) animal (M + L + C, or matter with life with consciousness); and (4) human (M + L + C + SA, or matter with life with consciousness and with self-awareness, or the power to direct our consciousness in accordance with our purposes).

Schumacher then says,

> In a hierarchy structure, the higher does not merely possess powers that are additional to and exceed those possessed by the lower; it also has power *over* the lower. It has the power to organize the lower. . . . Are there powers that are higher than self-awareness? Are there levels of being above the human? . . . . The great majority of mankind throughout its known history . . . has been unshakenly convinced that the chain of being extends upward beyond man. This universal conviction of mankind is impressive for both its duration and its intensity. Those individuals of the past whom we still consider the wisest and greatest not only shared this belief but considered it of all truths the most important and the most profound.

He goes on to point out that each level of being is profoundly more *aware* and more active (less passive) than the level below it. . .'. But even at the human level a great deal of unawareness, passivity, and dependency remain. "Observing this," says Schumacher, "mankind has always used its intuitive powers to complete the process, to extrapolate the observed curve to its completion. Thus we conceive a being, *wholly* active, *wholly* sovereign and autonomous; a person above all merely human persons.

The four levels of being are thus seen as pointing to the . . .
existence of a level (or levels) of being above 'the human.' "

A higher awareness exists that can enlighten and expand
our own awareness and produce the flashes of insight to
which most scientists and discoverers attribute their clearest understandings. Whether it is categorized as a religious
belief or simply as a sense of some source of insight and
awareness beyond our own, regardless of our personal terminology or theology or perspective, most agree on two
points:

1. It is there.
2. We can tap into it.

This *superawareness* can help us to see more sharply
what is important and what simple things we could do to
make a difference. And it can help us discover serendipity
through a flash of insight or a new idea, or the "noticing" of
an unpredicted opportunity or need.

How do we tap in? How do we increase the frequency of
our flashes and expand our own awareness beyond the data
given to us by our five senses?

The answer is both so simple and so logical that it is easy
to overlook. The answer is to *ask*.

The most frequently repeated admonition, both in biblical scripture and in the writings of other world religions, is
the admonition to ask.

Whether a person has a clearly defined idea of God or an
extremely vague idea of some higher awareness, it stands to
reason that the greater comprehends and has interest in the
lower . . . and will respond to the lower's request for expanded awareness.

Ask for expanded awareness. Ask whoever you conceive the possessor of the greater awareness to be, or ask the awareness itself. Make the request as you sit down to work your triangle and decide on your three priorities or choose-to-dos each day, and ask it again and again in your mind as you live through each day.

In our family we have come to think of gratitude as such an important quality that Thanksgiving has become in many ways our favorite holiday. One tradition we have is to make a list each Thanksgiving morning, on a long roll of paper, of everything we can think of that we are grateful for. (Last year we listed over seven hundred things.) Then we have time contests to see who can read aloud through the whole list fastest.

We have also adopted the tradition of sending out a family Thanksgiving card each year instead of a Christmas card. It always contains a current picture of our family along with a poem about the current gratitude we feel.

Gratitude can and should be cultivated. It is not only a product of awareness, it is a precipitator of awareness. As we learn the art of gratitude, we become more aware.

The interchange between awareness and gratitude can extend to a deeper sensitivity to our relative position in the world and can make us grateful even for our problems.

One morning I (Linda) woke up feeling like my mind was in a vise. *How am I going to survive this day?* I thought. I had to help the children while they practiced, grab the boys before they got out the door without combing their hair, and write notes to teachers. I had to take a child to the dentist, get one child to work after school, another to a harp lesson, and another to Cub Scouts. I had to spend at least half the day at the office and to finish some writing for a newsletter. I had to find some place to put my preschoolers while I gave an art lesson at the sixth grade for the PTA, to fix dinner for ten, and to speak at a meeting in the evening. Then, after all that, I had to go to the airport and pick up a "new member" of our family—a twenty-two-year-old university student from mainland China, whom we had agreed to sponsor and whose flight arrived at ten-thirty P.M.

Somehow I survived all the have-tos for the day. The next twenty-four hours with this young girl from another world taught me an important lesson that freed my mind from much of its stress. She told us that she had been assigned an occupation according to a test she had taken. She also said that families in China are limited to only one child and that the mother is allowed to stay home with that child for only one year before she must return to the factory and put her child in the factory nursery. This young lady's "upper class" family shared a living room with another family and was not allowed even to plant a tree without government permission.

Suddenly the hassles of my world looked like opportunities, the business like freedom, and the have-tos became choose-tos. I acknowledged that I had chosen my family size, my hectic schedule, and my demanding commitments. And I could choose to eliminate much of it—if I wanted to.

Decide to be more aware and to be more grateful. Work on it in your family and in your own mind and heart. Use a pen to help you. Write poetry about your awareness and diary entries about your gratitude. And return thanks to the source of superawareness, even as you ask that source for more light and for more insight.

The Speed of Going Slow

We've always wanted to invent a new comic book super-hero, who, rather than being extra strong and extra smart, simply had the power to slow time down so that everything and everyone around him was in slow motion, so that he was the only one who could move fast. In this situation he could speed past opponents to score or win in any sport, he could easily block any attack on himself, he could even catch bullets in midair.

A lot of us wish for something like that. And since we can't slow things around us down, we try to speed ourselves up. We hurry, we rush, we hustle. We run ourselves ragged trying to get ahead . . . or to stay even . . . or to catch up.

And then occasionally we encounter one of those puzzling individuals who seems to have time for everything, and for everyone. He doesn't hurry. He doesn't seem impatient or rushed. It almost seems like he's got nothing to do . . . yet he gets so much done!

Think about something: Stressed people are always in a hurry. People in a hurry are always stressed. People who don't hurry aren't frustrated. People who aren't frustrated don't hurry. Which is cause and which is effect? Does hurry cause stress or does it result from it?

Could it be that we are more like our potential comic-book character than we think? Could it be that our attitude and our approach to life actually affect how fast our time passes? Perhaps we are a little like gerbils on a treadmill who, by running faster and faster, succeed only in making their world spin around them faster. And perhaps, conversely, when we relax, when we consciously slow ourselves down and become a little more patient, a little more observant and sensitive—perhaps then we actually slow down our time treadmill and find ourselves able to do more by hurrying less.

One thing is for sure: When we slow down and center ourselves, we begin to see more; and part of what we see may be a shortcut, or a better way, or even a better place to be or a better thing to do. We begin to think more when we slow down, and thinking usually saves time. We begin to be more aware of what is really important. And we start to notice what is unimportant—enough so that we can abbreviate it or even eliminate it.

One year part of our family Thanksgiving card was about the speed of going slow:

Can words describe this sense, so seldom obtained?
So soft, so simple.
Time for people, inner peace enough
to look into eyes with interest—
instead of self-consciousness.
Time to wait—and let things come to you
instead of going after them.
More time, slower time.
The curious, calm capacity to enjoy simply,
to think freely, to feel deeply.
A slow, sweet sensation, a stillness inside.
You feel the ground through the soles of your shoes
and the sky all around you.
A feeling like ripples, gentle and easy across vast depth.
Sometimes it comes after a catharsis,
after four or five days of vacation,

trying to relax, finally slowing down.
Sometimes it just comes, unexpectedly, perfectly,
for no apparent reason except
maybe you slowed down, looked around,
liked what you saw;
or maybe you asked for it, believing that it can come as a gift
from a spirit far deeper than your own.

For Mother's Day last year the children gave me (Linda)
a treasure. Our fourteen-year-old, a gifted artist, had drawn
a caricature of each family member, and above each head
was a little balloon (cartoon style) with that person's most
common "saying." All the children had helped to fill in the
balloons.

The comments ranged from "I'm telling" above the head
of our ten-year-old tattler to "I'm not your little servant!"
above the head of our three-year-old (which is what he says
every time anyone asks him to do something). Apparently
they could not limit themselves to just one comment from
me, because above my head were four little balloons containing the following sayings: "Where are your shoes?"
"Where is my purse?" "Do your homework!" and "Get in
the car, we're late!" (Notice there was nothing like "Come
here, you sweet little thing, and let me kiss you.")

It was that fourth balloon above my head which struck
me most forcefully. I pride myself on being on time, and yet
I know that when I start hurrying and get hassled, time
seems to speed up and I get irritable, say things I don't
mean, break things, back the car into posts, and generally
become hard to be around. The children's message inspired
me to set a goal for the next month—a goal to slow down—
even if it caused me to be late for a few things. With the

goal in mind, I succeeded in moving and thinking more deliberately and was amazed at how often I got more done and arrived early for commitments.

That and other experiences like it have convinced me that there is a "speed" in going slow. It is still a struggle to keep myself from pushing the kids out the door and yelling, "Get in the car, we're late!" but I'm working on it.

"Slow down, you move too fast. You've got to make the morning last," says Simon and Garfunkel's "Fifty-Ninth Street Bridge Song." Other songs tell us to "Take time to smell the roses" and to live in the present—to live "Today while the blossom still clings to the vine." The lyrics reach us somehow, touching some inner place in us that knows that hurry never works and that we miss so much if we move too fast. Another song, from the Roger Miller score of Broadway's *Big River,* warns against becoming one of "the hasty hard to know" and advises us to "just lie and let your feelings grow accustomed to the dark, and by morning's light you just might know the feelings of the heart."

When we teach ourselves to slow down, we are also teaching ourselves to feel more, to notice more, to be more sensitive and tuned in to other people. The slowdown brings with it a contagious calm. We find that our work makes more sense, our problems yield to solutions, and our children magically are more peaceful, easier to manage, and inclined to give us spontaneous kisses and hugs.

Our kids have four all-time favorite movies—videos they have played so often they're nearly worn out. We didn't think they had anything particular in common until we happened to think about them while we were writing this chapter. They are *Chariots of Fire, The Black Stallion, The Man from Snowy River,* and *The Princess Bride.* Each of them portrays a certain *calm* and takes the time to focus and dwell on the beauty of the moment. The lead character in each film is patient and rather peaceful, able to think and reflect and observe—to respond calmly to whatever challenge arises. The tone in each case is the opposite of hurry.

Slow time down by slowing yourself down. The more you succeed in doing this, the *longer* your life will be.

Playfulness and Humor

"The reason angels can fly," said G. K. Chesterton, "is that they have learned to take themselves lightly." Most of us have not learned this ability. As a result we are a lot less like "the angels" than we are like Woody Allen's self-description. "Most of the time I don't have much fun," said Allen, "and the rest of the time I don't have any fun at all!"

One morning I (Linda) stomped into the kitchen while all the children were sitting at the breakfast table. I was absolutely furious about how the day had gone thus far. No one had done anything that should have been done. No beds were made, no music practiced, homework assignments were not ready, and these chattering little "good-for-nothings" dared to be giggly at the breakfast table as though it were just another day!

Smoke must have been curling out of my ears as I, pregnant and hormone-laden, began yelling at the kids—uncharacteristically loud and menacing. Some looked shocked, others amazed, one maybe even a little frightened. But one with big brown eyes and a grin on his face began to giggle.

"Noah, don't you *dare* laugh at me when I'm this angry.

You're taking your life in your hands!" I screamed. Seven-year-old Talmadge leaned his head over on ten-year-old Saydi's shoulder and began laughing, too. It was as though someone had turned on the laughing gas. They were all tittering—as though they were watching a funny movie.

I experienced a brief moment of insight, seeing myself as I looked to them, and realized that they *were* watching a funny movie—starring *me!* It wasn't easy, but I took one step back and looked the situation over and managed to crack a smile and a little giggle myself.

We all know that the old formula, crises + time = humor, is true. In hindsight I'd like to add that the shorter the time element is, the better . . . for everyone's mental health.

Life in a crisis-ridden existence can certainly be lighter and funnier and more enjoyable if we look at the world not through rose-colored glasses but through humor-tinted glasses.

Having fun, taking ourselves lightly, playfulness, humor. How important are they? We're told by doctors that laughter is the best cure for ulcers. A good laugh, it seems, secretes a chemical in our stomachs that aides digestion. Dr. Norman Cousins claims with great credibility that he cured his cancer with a regimen of laughter (which, among other things, involved watching old Laurel and Hardy and Three Stooges movies).

Humor and playfulness not only refresh our own sense of perspective and aid our health and well-being, they also have an obvious positive effect on others. They cheer people up and take their minds off their troubles.

We have a nine-year-old who decided that he wanted to be a doctor. (His desire stemmed partly from the friendship he's developed with our family doctor through having been stitched up and put in casts so many times. This boy is so interested in the medical process that he's almost pleased when one of his frequent injuries occurs.)

One day we asked him why he thought he'd be such a good doctor. "Well," he said, "for one thing blood doesn't make me sick at all! And for another thing I'm pretty good at telling jokes, so I can keep people's minds off their hurts."

Someone who has a goal of smiling more will suddenly find the people around him smiling more, too. Fun is not a childish pursuit—but it is contagious.

Humor is related in a most interesting way to service and empathy. Each of the qualities depends on observation and awareness. People who are empathetic and service-oriented are able to be that way because they observe and clearly see the situations and needs of other people. Humor also comes from awareness—from noticing the little ironies and quirks of life—and from seeing the universality of the human predicament. Next time you listen to a stand-up comedian, realize that he's talking about very ordinary things that he sees in an extraordinary and perceptive way. In this sense humor is also related to poetry. Both the comic and the poet see things in ordinary life that the rest of us miss.

Somewhere inside we all want to be more playful—and we know that the playfulness is in us . . . somewhere.

I (Richard) was lecturing at a large insurance association seminar. The speaker who had preceded me was a noncon-formist type of fellow whose subject was "having fun." He came into the hall (where everyone was wearing business suits) in a pair of cords and a lumberjack flannel shirt. He started out his presentation by asking, "All right, what do you people do for fun?" After a short, awkward silence a couple of people raised their hands. One played tennis, but as the speaker questioned him, it became obvious that tennis was a very competitive ego thing for him and not much fun at all. In the meantime the second person pulled her hand down.

After it had become clear that the audience really didn't do much of anything for fun, the speaker started telling us what *he* did. He always paid for his car *and* the car behind him at highway tollbooths so that he could watch in his rearview mirror the drama that unfolded when the driver behind him was told that his toll had been paid. He sent his favorite cartoons from *The New Yorker* to friends whom the cartoons reminded him of. When he traveled, he put little stick-on gold dots on airplane windows or on public phones or rest-room mirrors as a little game with himself so that he would remember that he had been there before if he ever got there again. Whenever he boarded a crowded elevator, he waited until the door closed and then turned to face the people and said, "You're probably wondering why I've called you all together here today."

Since I was the next speaker, I was seated on the stand, watching the audience. Their faces showed a mixture of dismay and admiration. They didn't really want to be impressed with this sort of craziness and nonsense, but they couldn't help being intrigued, and at least a little envious of someone who was simply having a lot more fun than they were.

The seminar was in British Columbia, and it happened that I had an extra day before my flight home. I was influenced by the "lumberjack"—enough that I used the day to go fishing. I kept the biggest fish I caught, froze it, wrapped it in plastic wrap, and carried it home in my briefcase. On the plane I found I was even more influenced by his idea of playfulness than I thought. A very bored flight attendant came by with her nasal, canned voice, saying, "Sir, would you prefer the braised tips of beef or the chicken cordon bleu?" Without stopping to think, I opened my briefcase and said, "Neither actually. I detest airline food, so I bring my own. Would you please cook this fish for me?"

Besides making us more alive, curing our ulcers, and making people around us happy, playfulness is a great way to escape boredom. Speaking of tollbooths, we are reminded of a day crossing the Bay Bridge between Oakland and San Francisco. Thirty-seven of the thirty-eight tollbooth attendants functioned like machines, taking money, giving change, sometimes saying "Thank you" for eight hours straight. The thirty-eighth tollbooth attendant was having fun. He had his boom box playing, and he practiced tap dancing (and sometimes singing) between cars.

"But I'm not funny, I'm not playful," you say. Well, why don't you be? It's your choice.

Is Anyone Too Spontaneous?

For every person who has become too structured and allowed planning to take away his or her flexibility there is another person who has far too little discipline, who is simply being swept along by the currents of life, seldom if ever setting a goal or preparing a schedule.

We had been giving *Lifebalance* Seminars for years, mostly to corporate and professional groups and almost exclusively to the type of overachievers who needed the spontaneity-serendipity-relationships emphasis of Lifebalance. Our audiences were too aggressive, too structured, too work oriented—and most of them knew it.

Then one pleasant week we flew to Hawaii to present *Lifebalance* to a large group of delightful Polynesians. Luckily our format involved lots of audience participation. If it hadn't, we probably would have gone right on preaching flexibility and antiplanning and taking-time-for-fun to people who had never set a goal or made a list in their lives! The fact that this audience was different from what we were used to started becoming clear to us when we asked, "How many of you use some kind of time-management tool or planner," and fewer than a dozen people out of five hundred raised their hands. It really became clear when we asked who knew what a time-management tool *was* and a man in the back row said that he thought it was some kind of extra-fancy socket wrench. It was an interesting afternoon. As it developed, we found that most of these people did know what planners were but couldn't imagine why they (or anyone) would use one.

"You do what needs to be done at the moment" was their attitude, "unless there's nothing that needs to be done badly, and then you do whatever you want."

"But what if there are so many things that need to be done that you don't have time to do them all?" we asked.

They looked at us, looked at each other, and shook their heads a little—trying to understand what in the world we were talking about.

That day we took a whole new approach to Lifebalance. We ended up trying hard to convince the audience that there was some value in setting a few goals, and promising everyone there that the Lifebalance method would allow them do so *without* taking away their spontaneity or their wonderful ability to live in the present.

In today's world, setting no goals and making no plans for some people is simply a matter of culture. For others it is a matter of laziness. Still others avoid goal setting out of a conscious fear of responsibility or because they don't want to make their shortcomings more obvious to themselves. But for many it is a matter of choice based on a decision to value spontaneity and flexibility and not to kill either with too much structure.

We frequently open *Lifebalance* Seminars the way we did that day in Hawaii—by asking our audience how many use time-management or planning books. In more typical audiences lots of hands go up, and normally about half of the audience is anxious to tell how much they depend on their planning system and how much it has done for them.

Then we ask how many intentionally *don't* use detailed planners, and why. We ask what the potential drawbacks and disadvantages of these tools can be. And it is like opening a floodgate.

The other half of the audience suddenly has something to say. "Lists and planners take away your spontaneity." "They set you up to fail." "They make you worry." "They make you stiff and insensitive." "They cause you to be too aware of all the things you should have done."

Most people have come to think of it as an either-or question. Either you schedule and structure everything and make yourself into a machine or you stay free and spontaneous and sensitive.

Getting both sides from the audience sets the stage for us to explain Lifebalance—to try to persuade half of our audience to adopt serendipity and be free from their schedules once in a while, and to persuade the other half that daily goals and priorities can be set in a balanced way and can be *combined* with awareness and sensitivity.

Remember that the goal is balance. At the heart of balance lies the understanding that a little structure is good for spontaneity—and a little flexibility is good for discipline.

When, Then or Now?

Goal setters tell us to project ourselves into the future. Poets tell us to live in the present. Genealogists and historians extol the benefits of the past. How should you orient your life? Is it best to live in the future, the present, or the past?

Be careful! The question establishes another dangerous set of false alternatives, another choice we should *not* make, another time when we are wiser to choose the answer "all of the above."

The past, the present, and the future are not opponents or competitors; they are teammates. They are different generations of the same family; they are interdependent cogs in the same machine. And they can be great friends— friends that assist each other, learn from each other, and teach each other.

One day when our first child was nearly a year old, I (Linda) remember thinking, "Won't it be great when this child can walk? . . . I'm breaking my back carrying her everywhere."

Saren was one of those children who learned to walk all

of a sudden, and just a couple of weeks later I caught my-self saying, "Wasn't it great when this kid stayed in one place?"

The "Won't it be great!/Wasn't it great!" syndrome af-fects all of us to some degree. The medicine for it is not to quit thinking about the future or the past, or even to quit thinking about how wonderful they will be or were. The medicine is to add, in the same breath, how great (or at least how interesting) the present is also.

Instead of longing for the good times of the past, be content simply to remember them with relish. Instead of being impatient for the future to come, enjoy the process of planning how you want it to be. Learn to see the present as that one focused moment when you can actually do things rather than remember them or plan them.

The fact is that you can live in the future, the past, and the present all at once. The best way to learn how to do so is to get three books of blank paper. Label one of them "The Past," and use it as your diary. Whether you write in it daily, weekly, or just periodically, concentrate on things you have learned, things you have felt, and the progress you have made. If you've never kept a diary before, try to catch up by dividing your past life into eras separated by major changes, moves, or milestones in your life. Then write (or tape-record and transcribe) everything you can remember about each era.

Label your second book "The Present." Use it as a way to enhance your awareness of "the now." Write poetry or short essays about your observations, about beauty or something of particular intrigue you have noticed, about your experi-ences of the moment.

Call the third book "The Future," and use it to plan the

future eras of your life—to set goals for who and where and what you want to be at certain dates that lie ahead.

I (Linda) thought that what I wanted more than anything in the world was another driver in our family—someone to help me get everybody where they were supposed to be during the week. I counted the days until our oldest daughter turned driving age the way a child counts the days until Christmas.

We turned her over to a driving school to get the required certificate to apply for a license. A few days before Saren took her driving test, I went out with her. To my horror I realized that Saren was unsafe at any speed.

Her response to my distress was, "Mother, if you gasp for breath one more time, I am going to scream. You are making me *sooooo* nervous."

She did get her driver's license—much to my amazement. But on Saren's first time out alone, I found myself back in the "remember when" syndrome. "Wasn't it nice when I didn't have to worry about this!"

Our goal should be learning to live simultaneously in the past, the present, and the future, and learning to think of the three as friends of ours as well as friends of each other.

Use a mountain-climber metaphor: Enjoy looking up at the peak you intend to climb. Enjoy looking back at the view of where you've been. And enjoy the feel of rocks through your soles as you take each step through the present.

Taking Risks and Following Feelings

We know a tennis instructor who is always saying to his students, "Take risks! You won't hit many winners unless you go for it and risk hitting the ball out. And the real joy in tennis is not winning, it's hitting winners."

Life is much the same. Avoiding risk, never trying anything we are unsure of, always taking the easy, known route, staying with something you've done repetitively for years—such "safe" approaches to life lead to neither joy nor progress. The real joy in life lies not in months or years or accumulated security but in moments—the moments when we take risks and allow ourselves to feel.

Incidentally this same sports coach also teaches skiing. You can guess what he says to his pupils on the hill. "Don't be afraid to fall down. When you fall down, it's proof that you're trying to go beyond what you could do before. If you're not falling down, you're not learning."

We were at a San Diego beach not long ago, early one morning, watching joggers and beach walkers. To avoid the waves and keep their feet dry, some walked high up on the beach, slogging through the loose, dry sand. Others risked the waves, running low and close to the breakers on the firm, smooth, wet sand. In life the firmest, fastest footing where the greatest progress is possible is near the waves of risk.

Risk in this sense is not a synonym for foolishness or casual disregard for danger. Risk is valuing progress and uniqueness more than you fear failure or ridicule. Theodore Roosevelt said it this way: "In the battle of life, it is not the critic who counts. . . . The credit belongs to the man who is actually in the arena . . . who, if he succeeds, knows the triumph of high achievement; and if he fails, at least fails while daring (risking) greatly, so that his place will never be among those cold and timid souls who never knew either victory or defeat."

A close friend of ours, for years an eminent university professor, has always been concerned about what he calls "too high a comfort level." He likes this quote: "There is no progress in passing from ease to ease." Some time ago he began to feel that his tenured position, his teaching the same classes year after year, the respect and acceptance he enjoyed among students and other faculty—all these were raising his comfort level much too high. So he quit. He left the university and started other pursuits. Each of these pursuits was new, each was less secure, but each involved the kind of risk that he felt made him more alive.

Botanists tell us that seeds, just before they burst into growth, begin to vibrate rapidly. People, before they begin to grow, begin the shaky process of taking risks.

Another friend, one I (Richard) have known since grade school, invites me once a year for a long walk and talk in a mountaintop forest near our childhood home. The talks are always candid. We give each other a type of feedback that would be impossible between people who didn't know each other well or who had known each other for less time. One year my friend said something to me that I'm not sure was intended totally as a compliment. I took it as one, though, because it dealt with something which I felt so strongly about, particularly since I had been thinking about and working on *Lifebalance*. "You have always been," my friend said, "interested in doing *different* things, and in doing them in a *different* way. You want to do things differently than others do them—and differently than the way you have ever done them before."

Someone said, "Think of life as a constant struggle not to be influenced." Part of taking risks is daring to do different things in a different way. It is saying, "I know that is the ordinary thing to do, but why be ordinary?" It is saying, "I know that is the usual way of doing it, but I'm not sure it is the best way," or "I'm not so sure there is one 'best way.' "

This kind of thinking always involves the risk of criticism or jealousy. But you can comfort (and compliment) yourself with Einstein's quote: "Great spirits have always encountered violent opposition from mediocre minds."

Risk is related to feeling. Those who learn to relish rather than fear a certain amount of risk are more alive and feel more than those who avoid risk. Taking risks is one of the ways we can teach ourselves to feel.

e. e. cummings said, "A poet is someone who feels and puts these feelings into words. Most people think or believe or know that they can feel, but that is thinking, or believing, or knowing—not feeling. Anyone can be taught to think or believe or know, but not a single human being can be taught to feel!"

It is an intriguing and beautifully expressed statement. But it is *wrong*. People can be taught to feel. If not by others, they can teach themselves. One way to learn how to feel is to take risks. Another way (an ironic one in light of what cummings said) is to try to write poetry—to try to probe our hearts, first asking ourselves what we feel and then trying to express it.

Depth of feeling is often in direct proportion to effort extended. Exerting ourselves physically causes us to feel tired but also strengthens our endurance. Mental effort allows us to feel both the fatigue and the exhilaration of observation and learning. Extending ourselves emotionally leads to deeper feelings and greater capacity to care and to love.

There is a particular type of feeling that we often call impressions, hunches, intuition, or nudges. Following them involves an interesting type of risk. In a world so oriented to hard processed data, information systems, logic, and objective proof, there seems little place for something as subjective as a feeling or a hunch, and taking a "prompting" or a "nudge" too seriously can feel emotionally and perhaps socially risky. It's safer, and more common, to put intuition in the same category as superstition, horoscopes, or fortune-telling. After all, we are modern, scientific people, and any data not received objectively through one of our five senses is suspect.

Yet perhaps it is less suspect now than even five years ago. More and more of us, it seems, as we face a new millennium are coming to believe that carefully tuned intuitive feelings are often *more* reliable than sight, hearing, touch, taste, or smell. And we are finding that the "non-process" of intuition can be at least as useful as the process of logic.

When promptings and nudges are ignored or discounted, they come less frequently. They feel like unwelcome strangers. When we stop trusting our feelings, we also stop valuing them. We stop welcoming feelings and we stop cultivating them. And pretty soon they stop coming.

People who stop feeling, in a sense, stop living.

Notions and impressionistic feelings resemble radio signals in that they become stronger when they are carefully tuned into. The way to tune in on feelings is to notice them, appreciate them, probe and try to feel their full depth, and then act on them.

Certain feelings resemble radio signals in another way. They come from an external source. There are soft, still, sure feelings that tell us things we know are correct but can't trace by logic or cause and effect. There are feelings of beyond-self strength that sometimes come when we meet an obstacle bigger than we can handle. Especially at the moment we are having them we are aware that these feelings come into us from without . . . from some intelligence far greater than our own. And we sense that that source feels for us and is responsive to our requests.

A dear British friend of ours, a remarkably accomplished and thoughtful man who is a member of Parliament and an acclaimed educator, believes in (and attributes his own best thoughts and strengths to) a "highly superior intelligence" who has set up for us some sort of "access circuitry" to which we can "plug in" by asking and by listening in our minds.

Scott Peck, in his runaway best-seller, *The Road Less Traveled*, expresses belief in "a personal, loving God whose objective is to help us become as He is."

Whether an individual's personal beliefs resemble Peck's or the Parliament member's, it is completely logical to believe that the greater intelligence is both willing and able to assist our lesser intelligence.

Human beings are equipped with great capacity for intuition and feelings, and with the ability, when they look deep inside themselves, to know which of these feelings come from (or are confirmed by) a greater and wiser source. In this context we must try never to ignore our intuition and impressions, particularly when it feels they are coming to us from a higher, clearer source.

Make friends with your feelings. Welcome them and nurture them. Take the time (and the risk) to let them sink deeper inside and to follow where they lead. Learn to frequently ask yourself not only how you feel but *what* you feel. Become good at asking the questions—and good at answering them—and at finding your own way to pray for the answers beyond.

Implementing Attitude Balance

"JUMPING THE LINE" AND "RIGHT-BRAIN RETENTION"

Another Daily and Weekly Habit

Okay, let's say you agree that you want to "get there" *and* "enjoy the journey," that you want to "act" *and* "respond," that you want to develop and use the intuitive right hemisphere of your brain *and* the logical left, that you want to ride in jet planes *and* hot-air balloons, to be both structured *and* spontaneous, both disciplined *and* flexible.

Is "wanting" this kind of balance enough?

No!

Not nearly enough. Deep down we all want the balance; we all want both sides. But achieving this balance of mind and attitude requires a particular and fresh new way of thinking. We need some new mental exercises that train our minds to go in both directions.

It's one thing to understand what you want and another thing to do it. It's one thing to know the type of person you want to be and another thing to become that type of person. It's one thing to believe or accept the principles—the ideas and ideals of attitude balance—and another thing to implement them.

There is a daily exercise that can become a habit that can change the way we see and the way we do things and that can make us better at discipline and achievement even as it helps us become more sensitive, more spontaneous, and more flexible.

The habit involves two things: (1) something called serendipity lines and (2) a new definition of a perfect day.

A serendipity line is simply a centered top-to-bottom line that divides a daily-planning page in half. The day's schedule (which should include the *family, work,* and *self* choose-to-dos from the priority blanks at the top of the page) is written on the left of the line.

The right-hand side of the page is left blank as a simple acknowledgment of the fact that many things will occur during the day that were *not* planned. There will be unanticipated needs, unforeseen opportunities, unexpected moments of beauty. There will be things to be responded to and to be enjoyed. They will not be things you could have planned (i.e., your planner will never say, "3:30—get a new idea," or "4:30—get a call from an old friend," or "6:45—watch a beautiful sunset"). These things will happen, but we never know when, and the goal is to notice them and capture them. As Walpole intimated, everyone is exposed to unexpected opportunities, needs, and beauties, but these are far more *noticed* by those who (1) are purposefully pursuing something—usually something *else* and (2) are sagacious (observant and wise) enough to notice.

If you have goals and a plan for the day, then when you notice a possibility you had not planned, you are in a position to *choose* whether to stay with what you had planned or to "jump the line" and do the serendipity thing instead.

The suggested habit, then, involves one little addition to the daily planning and "working the triangle" already presented in the last section. The addition is the serendipity line. Plan and schedule on the left and let the blank right side remind you to notice, to appreciate, to respond, to take risks, to be playful and spontaneous—in short to be *serendipitous*. When you notice something better (or more needed) than what you had thought you would do, jump the line—decide to spend time on it instead of what you had planned to do. At the end of the day think back and write in your "serendipities" on the right side of your page. (Note: The things on the left side will be written in future tense, since they are plans and schedules. The entries on the right side will be in the past tense since you *responded* to them as they came up and made note of them *after* the fact.)

To make the habit work, you may need a new definition of a perfect day. Get rid of the idea that a perfect day is one in which you check or cross off every single thing you had planned to do. That might better be called a boring, robotlike day. Instead define the perfect day as one in which you accomplished most of the important things on the left side of your line but managed to jump the line two or three times to do serendipitous things.

What happens on the right-hand side is often at least as important as what goes on on the left. "Serendipities" usually fall into one of five categories: *needs, opportunities, people, ideas,* or *beauties*. They may be small needs, small beauties, small ideas. But the fact that they are small doesn't mean they are unimportant.

There is a second habit, a monthly one, that can enhance your ability to jump the line and that can help you keep track of the happy surprises and serendipities that have entered your life. It is called *right-brain retention,* and it assists in the effort to live in the future, the present, and the past. It works like this: Once a month, during your half-hour saw-sharpening on Sunday, go back through your daily plans and extract or index the things from the right-hand side that you want to retain or keep track of. (While you're at it, index the important things from the left side of the line, too.)

The easiest way to do this is to make a simple monthly index of the needs, opportunities, people, ideas, or beauties (N, O, P, I, or B) that you have noted on the right (seren-dipity) side. The index for each month would probably consume less than a page and might start like this:

B   June 2—exceptional sunset

P   June 3—met Jeff Kramer

N   June 3—played catch with Billy, talked about
        school problem

O   June 4—saw special sale on lawn mowers

I   June 5—ideas for disciplining teenagers from
        Pat

N   June 6—helped Harry understand inventory
        system

O   June 6—idea for joint marketing project on new
        product

From this index you can locate and review the notes you made on the right-hand side of a particular day in your planner.

Taking fifteen minutes—perhaps on the first Sunday of each month—to perform the right-brain retention and to "inventory" your serendipity for the month just past is an educational and worthwhile habit. It will not only help you retain, use, and follow up on the surprises and opportunities that have come along, it will make you more aware and appreciative of the value of the unplanned things in life. You will very likely realize that the things on the right side are as important if not more valuable and important than the planned things on the left-hand side. Thus the inventory will strengthen your commitment to serendipity.

Goal Balance

BALANCING ACHIEVEMENTS WITH RELATIONSHIPS

Conceptualized, Pleasurable Desire

"Goals"
Definition: "Things I want to achieve."
Two problems:
1. *Things:* Most of us have too many already . . .
Where are *people*?
2. *Achieve:* Are what we can put on a resume
(accomplishments)
As important as what we can't (relationships)?
A better definition: "A conceptualized, pursuable *desire*."
A clear picture of something the way we desire it to be.
A big new house, a fat salary, a corner office.
Sure . . .
But what, in your clearest, best self
Do you desire more?
Love,
Peace,
Deep, committed relationships and
True, honest character?
But are these the stuff of goals?
Yes and no.

No, they usually are not,
Yes, they should be, and yes, they can be.
A new *kind* of goals,
Still a picture of the future,
But not a picture of things—
One of people, love, communication, trust,
Commitments kept,
Character built.
A picture in your mind *now,* of a relationship
The way you want it to be *then*.

The third type of balance is *goal balance*.

Goals or objectives are generally thought of in association with relationships, and with becoming and giving. It is
not necessary to choose between people and things—but
to avoid the choice, we must develop the ability to balance.

People and Things

One busy weekend as I (Linda) prepared a big Sunday
meal, my four-year-old helper, Noah, who was sitting on
our kitchen bar, inadvertently kicked a china bowl onto the
floor. Richard had hand-carried that particular fine bone
china bowl all the way from England, and he became
uncharacteristically angry when he saw the smashed re-
mains.

"Go straight to your room, Noah, and think about why it
was that you knocked that bowl off with your foot," he
demanded. "You know better than to climb up there on the
bar!"

Obediently Noah left, weeping and wailing. Five minutes later, having recovered his usual feistiness, he came back and looked up into his daddy's face. "What's more important," he said indignantly, "the bowl or me?"

What matters?

It's a question that runs through our minds fairly often in one form or another. But we don't usually think about it long enough or hard enough to answer it. And when we do answer the question, we find it hard to actively remember our answer long enough and consistently enough to implement it.

What matters is *people!*

People are usually less predictable than things. They are harder to manage, more exasperating, and they can hurt us more, or threaten us, disappoint us, or embarrass us. And people, if they are strangers with whom we have no connection, are much easier to leave alone than to get involved with.

But people are what count.

Achievements are hollow and mean little unless they help people and are *for* people. As the old adage says, "Why build these castles glorious if man unheralded goes? Nothing is worth the building unless the builder also grows."

A friend of ours who is a single parent told us once that for the first time in years she had a little extra money and some vacation time coming. She was trying to decide between the two alternatives of adding a second bathroom to her modest home or taking her three children on a family vacation. "We haven't been away together for years," she said, "but four people in one bathroom is ridiculous. I guess I'd better be practical, hadn't I?"

She sounded like she was trying to convince herself. We just listened and didn't offer much advice. We didn't see her for over a month, but when we did, she was beaming. "I did the practical thing," she said. We assumed she'd built the bathroom. But she went on, "We had the greatest trip. It's something we'll never forget. What memories we made! I've decided that the most practical things are the things that last the longest, and these memories will last forever!"

We lived for three years in England. In the first days and weeks after the move, it seemed so delightful to have a new form of privacy. Since we didn't know anyone socially, we had long, uninterrupted evenings at home. It was great for a while. But there came one evening when we felt so uninvolved and so bored that we decided simply to go out and meet the neighbors. The evening was remarkable. We felt the exhilaration of meeting new personalities, challenging ourselves to relate to them, getting interested in their interests.

We took the children along. On the way home our always-enthusiastic eight-year-old said, "Wow, we must have the most interesting neighbors in the world. I think meeting new people is the funnest thing there is." The six-year-old picked up in his own way on the idea. "I think we should always talk to people, even if they're weird."

There is a unique kind of excitement in a new relationship. And there is security and insight in old relationships. There is mutual benefit in friendly greetings or pleasant comments, even among strangers. Make the effort to say hello, to smile, to ask a thoughtful question, to pay a timely compliment, to start a conversation, and to constantly keep in mind the fact that people are more important than things.

L-Goals and R-Goals

"Goals." "Objectives."

Some people love the words because they conjure visions of fulfillment, power, and control. Others are made to feel tired and discouraged by their mere mention.

Whether they pick us up or puncture us, the words usually bring to mind lists of things to do, left-brain analyzing, logical planning, lightning-shaped check marks as action is taken.

L-goals, we could call them. Left-brain logic and lightning action applied to lists or accomplishment. L-goals are quantitative and measurable and can be built like Lego blocks into stepping-stone, staircase sequences in which short-term goals lead to long-term objectives.

"Get 'X' grade point average so that I can get into 'Y' university so that I can get 'Z' job and make 'A' money."

L-goals lend themselves to accomplishment—or to failure—and make either one more obvious (at least to the goal setter). They do help people get farther, faster, and fancier—and most complaints against them are born of laziness or personal frustration.

As long as they are our tools and our servants, L-goals are pluses. But when we give our devotion to them, to the extent that they become our masters, they begin to suck away our spontaneity, to force us away from flexibility, and to regulate us into the rigidity of robots.

But there is an antidote. It is called R-goals. Like an L-goal, an R-goal involves a vision of something as we want it to be. But R-goals are as different from L-goals as paintings are from mathematical equations.

R-goals are oriented to *relationships* rather than achievements, people rather than things. They involve *r*ight-brain ideas, intuition, and flashes of insight. They require *re*sponding and *r*eacting rather than controlling and manipulating.

R-goals are set by *imagining* a relationship the way you *want* it to be at some specific *future* point in time. R-goals become more real if they're written (as a *description* of a future relationship—with one's spouse, with a child, with a friend, with the self).

An R-goal is an image, complete with the feelings you want to attend the image. The image becomes reality not so much through careful planning or logical step-by-step implementation as through the subconscious "programming" that the image causes in our own minds. Once this self-programming is in place, we automatically (and almost in spite of ourselves) begin doing the things, behaving in the manner, and thinking and saying the words that cause our present relationships to take on the imagined qualities of the image in our mind.

L-goals are softened and controlled and kept in perspective by R-goals, and R-goals work best for a person who has the structure and discipline of L-goals. In short, balance requires both.

One Sunday night, early in our marriage, I (Richard) sat down in our little student-housing apartment in Cambridge, Massachusetts, to review my goals. I had begun the practice of Sunday sessions and had become a strong believer in the power of clearly set and vividly imagined goals.

That evening I reviewed my financial goals. I reviewed my career goals. I reviewed the goals I had set for getting the next promotion at work, for buying our first home, for getting in better physical shape, for learning to play the cello. I reread my calculation of what I wanted to have (and what I wanted to have done) in five years, then I went over what I had to do this year to be on course and in sync with the longer-range goals.

The sun was setting on a lovely autumn day. I looked up from my papers and planners and gazed out on the sun's last light reflecting on the Charles River. My mind drifted and daydreamed, and I found myself thinking that the most important things in my life were not the ambitions and objectives written on the pages in front of me. The important things were Linda, our new baby, my friends, my extended family. The most valuable things in my life were *relationships*.

So why didn't any of my goals relate directly to the improving and perfecting of these relationships?

The reason, I mused, was that relationships couldn't be quantified or measured. One couldn't very well say, "I have a ten-year goal of a perfect relationship with my wife, so my five-year goal is to have a fifty-percent perfect relationship with her." Relationships, by their very nature, do not lend themselves to measurable goals or objectives.

But the golden evening outside became even more beautiful, and I kept gazing and kept thinking. I realized that the mind, when it could envision something, could lead you to it. If you wanted As on your next semester's transcript, you had to write down the goal—conceive it and believe it—and then your mind would tell you, sometimes consciously and sometimes subconsciously, what you had to do to achieve it. Essentially goals were clear mental images of things as you wanted them to become. So why couldn't they work with relationships?

Because relationships are harder to imagine and to describe than things or achievements. It's easier to "see" As on a future report card, or a certain amount of money in the bank by a certain date, than it is to imagine something as complex as a relationship in the form that you would like it to be at some future time.

Yes, it is harder, but it isn't impossible, and relationships are worth whatever effort they require.

I ended up sitting in that same chair most of the night. I wrote a description of the relationship I wanted to have with Linda five years from that date. I described the trust we would have between us, the confidence we would feel in each other, and the things we would each do for the other. The description also prompted me to write a list called "Linda is . . . ," which reviewed what I knew about her makeup and her nature, and another list called "Linda needs from me . . . ," which grew naturally out of the way I was thinking about her.

Silver moonlight had now replaced the sun on the river outside, but once I started, I couldn't stop. I wrote a description of the relationship I hoped to have with our baby daughter by the time she was six years old, enjoying the imagination involved in thinking what she might be like, and trying to project what kind of father I wanted to be to her and the way in which I hoped she would think of me.

I decided the "relationship goals" would become a part of my Sunday sessions, that I'd keep them entirely private in the back of my journal, that I would take a few minutes each week to review my written descriptions, perhaps to add to them or modify them, and to think about my progress toward them.

Balance the L-goals of your life with some R-goals. Setting them will tax your imagination and test your writing ability, but the process itself will put your priorities in order, and your descriptions of future relationships will give you a hopeful, almost magnetic vision of the future and will refresh your perspectives of what really matters in life.

Giving Things Up Mentally

Now that we've talked about *recognizing* and *acknowledging* relationships as more important than achievements (and people as more important than things), the question is, does it really have to be a choice? Is it either-or? Must we choose between being thing-oriented and being people-oriented? Are achievers necessarily insensitive to relationships? Does the accumulation of things have to cause us to care more about things than about people?

These are tricky questions. A rather strong case can be made for the answer yes. (Yes, it is a choice. Yes, financial or career achievements get in the way of relationships. Things often supersede people.) There are some solid spokesmen to back up this view. Thoreau felt that the anti-thing simplicity of a Walden Pond was necessary to maximize his relationship with God and self. Gandhi gave up all worldly possessions but his eyeglasses and scriptures. The New Testament tells us that "a double-minded man is unstable in all his ways," that men cannot serve "both God and Mammon." Contemporary writers such as Duane Elgin, author of *Voluntary Simplicity,* tell us that we should give up fancy food and modern conveniences in sympathy for those in the world who have neither. For centuries people have entered monasteries and deprived themselves of all but the most basic necessities and of any worldly recognition in order that they might reach deeply into themselves and see into the hearts of others.

But there is another view. It is the view that sees both things and achievements as the *means* to *ends* that involve people and relationships. It is the notion that says, "Yes, I could give up my indoor plumbing in order to be more basic and humble and to better appreciate the plight of the poor, but then I would have to spend a lot of time pumping and carrying water—and I may be able to do something more useful for myself and for others with that time."

It is possible to accept the Bible's admonition and the examples and teachings of the Thoreaus and Gandhis of the world and to follow them mentally in our *attitudes* and *priorities* and *perceptions*—without throwing away everything that we have and living on the exposed side of a mountain. It is possible to change ourselves radically on the inside without starting over on the outside. It is possible to view our means as the provider of freedom—freedom that can be used to cultivate relationships and to help other people.

Individuals who have idealistically given up all possessions usually did so as a means of changing themselves *inside*. The process can work in reverse. As we impress ourselves with the *truth* that things don't matter, that achievements are of no real value unless they help people, we begin to change how we think, and *external* changes in how we live are sure to follow.

A friend who was staying with us received two bits of very bad news in the same day. The first was a phone call from his broker telling him that a major investment had experienced major losses. The second message also came by phone, this time from the person who was house-sitting his home, letting him know that his new, still uninsured car had been stolen.

He was a little shaken, but not much. "They're just things," he said. "They can be replaced. Except for your family and your health, you really can't lose anything very important."

An attitude like that has several benefits. First, it eliminates an incredible amount of worry. Second, it simplifies life by keeping us from having or even wanting a lot of material things that we don't need. Third, surprisingly, it helps us enjoy the things we do have more than we otherwise would.

Think about that third point for a moment. At first thought it would seem that the more we cared about a thing, the more we would enjoy it. If something is very dear to us, if we worry about it and hoard it and try to protect it and keep it safe, then we will get more pleasure from it, right? The more we value it, the more we enjoy it, correct? No! It works that way with *people,* but not with *things.* Those who overvalue things are so busy protecting them and worrying about them that they rarely enjoy them. On the other hand those who see them only as things—things to be used, things to be appreciated, but things that could be replaced—these are the people who truly enjoy the things they have.

We get lots of practice giving things up mentally and physically at our house. With the number of children and their friends who are running in and out of our house, the chances are fairly good that new things, nice things, and expensive things as well as sentimental things and invaluable things (hardly ever the worthless things) will be bashed, scratched, broken, bent, crushed, or wrecked within a short time.

Kids tend to break and lose things, no matter how much we teach responsibility. The moving men drop our Steinway grand piano. The dogs ruin the new landscaping. The deer eat the pine trees in the winter. Spending a long time worrying about these kinds of accidents could drive one crazy in a very short time.

Scripture and wise philosophy do not tell us not to have things; they tell us not to *value* things. The admonitions are mental, not physical. We should not *treasure* the things of the earth that moths and rust can destroy and thieves can steal. We should not trade time for things. If someone asks for our coat, we should give him our cloak also. This is not to say we should not take good care of our things, but it is to say that we should not be preoccupied with possessions.

One way to deal mentally with the concept of possessions is to eliminate it, to adopt the belief that we can't really possess or own anything anyway. The earth and all the things in it belong to God. We may have use or *stewardship* of things, but sooner or later they pass on to others. We should want the use only of what we can take care of and enjoy.

Many make the error of mistaking wealth or imagined possessions for security. "I'm secure," they say, "because I've put lots away for a rainy day, because I have things." Real security is just the opposite. It is to be able to say, "I'm secure because I don't need any of those things. I could live without them. I am independent of them. If I lost them, I could replace them if I chose to." Security doesn't lie in the external "score" but in the internal attitude. A tennis player can be ahead but still be very much afraid that he will lose.

Another player may be behind, but quite secure in his knowledge that he has the ability to win (or that if he does lose, it's been good exercise, and there will be another day).

The attitudes we are speaking of here are not easily or quickly adopted, but with conscious effort they can be obtained. *Practice* not valuing things. Impress the attitude on yourself by repetition. Look for chances to demonstrate to yourself that things are tools to be used and enjoyed. Remind yourself that you're more interested in the things you need than in the ones you want, that you will quickly give up or give away a thing in favor of a person, and that it is *you* (rather than the world around you) who determines what you will value.

The rewards of your practice will be generosity, security, increased enjoyment, and a new perspective on almost everything.

Both!

People are more important than things, and relationships than achievements. When they conflict, the latter has to be given up (either physically or mentally) for the former. But we should reiterate that it usually doesn't have to be a choice. *Balance* has more to do with the words *both* and *blending* than it does with the words *either* and *or*.

Planning is often thought of as a science. And science, by definition, generally categorizes or separates things, divides apart and makes us choose between. One reason we call the Lifebalance kind of thinking antiplanning is that it is more an art than a science. Art tends to deal with combining things rather than with separating them.

One of the central challenges (and opportunities) of Lifebalance is mastering the art of consciously combining relationships with achievements—of blending people with things.

I (Richard) recall a particularly horrendous month! I'd been traveling much more than usual, and time with the children had been almost nonexistent. Then yet another unexpected (but "absolutely necessary") trip came up. After I stopped resenting it and looking for a way out, I started looking for a way *in,* or a way to combine. It was a trip to Arizona that involved one meeting and one television appearance. The airline had a "companion fare," and I realized it wouldn't be very expensive to take my two adolescent daughters along.

It was a Friday-to-Saturday trip, so they would miss only one day of school. (And they had a little saying: "Never let school get in the way of your education.")

It turned out to be a great experience. Alone with my two daughters, away from the distractions and obligations of home (and of their friends), we talked more in two days than we had in two months. One daughter, fascinated with media and production, had the time of her life at the studio, where the producer let her sit in the control booth. The other girl, interested in art and architecture, was fascinated by the style and decor of the interesting hotel where we stayed.

Instead of coming home feeling behind on my relationships, as I usually did, I felt "caught up."

It's not only big trips where we can take children along, and it's not only major, planned situations where we can think of and integrate our relationships with our work. Take a child shopping or on an errand. Get to know the person you're buying from or selling to and make a friend as well as a deal. Bring your spouse to the luncheon meeting or on a service call. Notice a fellow employee's personality, skills, and interests as well as the fact that he's competing with you for the same promotion.

People are naturally inclined toward setting up false alternatives in their minds, toward thinking in terms of either-or, toward choosing one thing at the expense of another. So often, with a little thought, *both* are possible. Separate options can work together, and even assist and enhance each other. Often, in the long run, life is more a question of "both or neither" than of "one or the other."

This "all or nothing"/"both or neither" principle is a particularly appropriate way of thinking about achievements and relationships. We can't be completely people oriented or totally thing oriented because true accomplishments always involve relationships, and the best relationships often grow out of worthwhile achievements.

Look for ways to integrate family, friends, and relationships into the achievements of your life. Think of the tasks and pursuits of the day not only as checkoffs on your list or stair steps to your goals—think of them as ways to make new acquaintances, as opportunities to work with others, and as chances to involve or learn from or serve people.

Nourishing Friendships

Some people collect rocks or stamps or coins. Others have learned to collect relationships and to cherish certain friendships that appreciate and grow in value more magically than the rarest antique.

Almost everyone has heard (and repeated) the Will Rogers quote: "I never met a man I didn't like." Something inside tells us that there is good in everyone, that there is something we can learn from everyone. "But there's no time," we say. "We don't even have time for the friends we already have." Yet collecting relationships doesn't take much extra time, it just takes a different attitude toward the people we meet every day.

Learning to view "incidental" people as interesting human beings and potential friends rather than as part of the scenery takes some real concentration. But there are at least two strong reasons for doing so (one very practical and one rather emotional):

1. People need people. A person you meet casually today may have a background, an ability, a capacity that you will need tomorrow. If you get to know a little about him, and if you remember him, he can become a *resource* that you may someday need. (The reverse is also true—he may need you and give you opportunities to serve or help.)

2. It is people—always people—who make life exciting. We are almost constantly surrounded by intrigue, by vast variety of experience, by diverse knowledge and insights of all kinds—in the form of the people around us. None of it flows to us without effort, but all of it is available to us if we learn to draw it out of the people who contain it. And our efforts to know others, to find out what they love or are good at, become the most motivating compliments we can give.

One summer while we were vacationing at a place called Bear Lake, in Idaho, we had an automobile accident. We hit a soft shoulder and bounced off a dirt road and through a fence into a boggy pasture. The bumps and bruises and the cast on a broken ankle kept us recuperating (and kept us grateful nothing more serious had happened) for a few days.

When things settled down, I (Linda) remembered the fence and realized that we ought to pay to have it repaired. We didn't have much of our vacation left, and I was a little irritated that I had to spend time worrying about replacing barbed wire. So I drove back to the scene of the accident— in a hurry—planning to take care of this detail as quickly as possible.

It was a beautiful, golden day—the first hint of autumn in the air—and as I drove, my mood mellowed. By the time I got there, I had let go of my hurry and remembered my goal of noticing people and collecting relationships. During the next hour I made friends with an interesting farm family, learned some fascinating things about the history of the lake, got some ideas about improving our own beach property, got our son (who had come along) involved in the friend-making conversation, and just generally had a great time—and, oh, incidentally, paid a small amount to cover some new barbed wire.

We so often think of people simply as objects who are part of (or sometimes barriers to) the things we want to get done. We need to reverse that and think of things and tasks as situations that will bring us into contact with people— people whom we can get interested in, learn from, identify with, and enjoy.

Start collecting relationships. In the same planner you use for daily planning, write down the people you meet each day—and what you learned about them, and what you learned from them, and what you liked about them. Review your notes at the end of the week in order to implant the new relationships into your memory. Take pride in moving toward a time when there are people you know and remember everywhere you go—relationships you have collected, friends you have made.

We have moved several times since we were married. Each time after we get the kids settled in schools and with friends, I (Linda) feel a longing for interaction with nourishing friends of my own.

Although Richard is my best friend, I always need "other mother" friends, who will know what I mean when I say, "Eli and his buddy played 'Singing in the Rain' with twenty pounds of unpopped popcorn in the storage room today."

In each new location I quickly try to organize what I call a mothers' group, which consists of four or five women whom I think of as "soul sisters" and with whom trivia is cut to a minimum so that we can talk about our kids, careers, ideas, books, stimulating people, and personal problems. We meet once a month and usually have a topic or a book to discuss.

As time has passed, women from the early groups have moved far away from each other. Yet to this day, because of the things we shared, any of us can pick up the phone and start where we left off—truly nourishing one another with our friendship.

Self-Programming, Solitude, and Relationship with Self

You can jog your brain while you're jogging your body—and it will make both respond better. An incident that occurred several years ago led to the idea of the "self-programming" method for improving the relationship with self.

I (Richard) passed our neighbor, George, one day while I was running. George was jogging around the same block but in the opposite direction. I said "hi," but George didn't seem to hear. It looked as if he was talking to himself. His lips were moving. The second time around the block, we met again. George *was* talking to himself.

"Helloooo, George," I said—loudly.

His eyes glanced up as we passed. "Morning," he said, still hardly seeing me.

The third time I stopped him. "George, what are you doing, building bridges while you run?" (George was a structural engineer.)

George looked up at me, out of the corners of his eyes (George is only five feet four inches). He was trying to decide whether to answer. After squinting up at me for a moment, he said, "Run the other way around the block with me and I'll explain."

George liked to answer questions with questions. He said, "Why do you run?"

I said, "To stay in shape, to live longer, to enjoy the fresh air."

George said, "Mmm, me too, but those are all secondary reasons for me. I jog to program my subconscious mind."

"To do *what*, George?"

"To self-program. What's happening while I jog is that I'm becoming a better person. I'm improving the way I relate to other people, and I'm making myself mentally stronger and more spontaneous."

George continued, between breaths, as we jogged together: "Most people spend all their time trying to change things outside of themselves. They are working for a new car, a new TV. They are trying to change their jobs, to raise their salaries. They are trying to change their wives or their children. Often they are well-meaning. They want to change something for the better."

George glanced over (and up) to see if I was listening. I was. He went on: "I think the thing we should be working on is ourselves. The thing we ought to be trying to change is us—the inside. The only real way to change other people or things is to change yourself. If you want to be a better father, you don't change your kids; you change yourself. If you want to do better at your job, you don't change your work; you change yourself. If you want to help the kids in the class you teach, you change yourself into a better teacher and a better example."

"That's very interesting, George, but what are you doing to change yourself while you are running?" George was excited now. He was huffing and puffing, but his voice had the tone of Columbus telling about his discovery of the new world.

"Doctors tell us—psychiatrists, too—that exercise not only opens up the heart and the circulation, it opens up the mind, clears the cobwebs, makes the brain more receptive to ideas, to what I call *self-programming*."

"What do you mean by that, George?"

"Well, you see, the subconscious mind is programmed by the input it receives. When I fail at something, my subconscious gets the message that I can't do it. When I hook the golf ball with my driver, my subconscious gets the message that I can't hit straight. But when I succeed at something, my subconscious gets a positive bit of programming. We are all our own creators in a way. What we do and think makes us what we are."

"Yes, but what about the running, George?"

"I'm getting to that. You see, the interesting thing about the subconscious is that it can't tell the difference between something that *happens* and something that is *thought*. And it can't tell the difference between something someone else says to it and something you say to it. So I pick things I'd like to be and I tell myself I already am! For example, while I'm running, I say to myself, "I am a spontaneous person. I notice unexpected beauty and unplanned opportunities." Then I think about evidence of this—how I noticed the clouds between the mountains last week, the surprise I found for my wife at the auction. My subconscious believes it. I become more of what I want myself to be."

I liked what George was saying, liked it enough that I began to try it myself. My own major priorities were Linda and the children. I decided to quit trying so hard to change them and instead use George's method to change myself— as a husband and as a father.

It was an interesting process. I identified some areas that I felt I needed to improve on, then refined them into a small number of *qualities* that I wanted to obtain—a half-dozen descriptive words that depicted the kind of husband and father I wanted to be. At first, as I jogged, I simply thought about each quality for a moment and tried to imagine settings and circumstances in which I could apply it. As time went by, I was able to think while I ran, of occasions when I had applied those qualities, and I was able to start using my symbolic words as descriptions of myself. For example, I would say to myself, *"Confidence.* I show *confidence* in my children. They feel my pride in them. I keep criticism and belittling out of my tone of voice and put *confidence* into my tone of voice. I look for chances to compliment them and to catch them doing something good. Yesterday I told Saydi how creative her school projects are, and I saw her take on the *confidence* I felt in her." Then I would say *"Consultant.* I try to be a *consultant* to my kids, not their boss or manager. This morning I didn't force or push Jonah to try out for the play. I just sat with him and helped him work out the pros and cons so that he could make his own decision."

Each morning when I ran, I went through each of my word-concepts. I soon became aware that I was exhibiting some of the qualities subconsciously, without thinking about them. I found that I was more aware of the children and of the teaching moments that presented themselves. Even though I was doing no more planning of specific activities and time with the children than I ever had, I was spending more time with them. It was better time, and it felt like less of a burden. I seemed to react instinctively with the answer or example they needed.

Pick out a few key adjectives that describe the type of person you want to be, the type of parent you want to be, the type of spouse you want to be. Create your own complete definitions for your chosen words, making those words symbolize the qualities you desire.

Then pick out some routine task or activity that you do

each day and use that time to think through your words—
and to program them into who you are.

Often the only privacy I (Linda) have during the day is a
few moments first thing in the morning in the bathroom.
That is where I do my self-programming. While there, I
also try to visualize the day. I don't have to wonder if there
will be a tense situation or crisis. I am absolutely sure there
will be. Knowing that I'll be walking into a "hurricane," I
resolve to be the "eye," the calm center of the storm that
swirls around me. I try to see myself responding kindly to a
screaming two-year-old, reasoning logically with a stubborn
ten-year-old boy, and ignoring outrageous statements by
teenagers. Sometimes I even rehearse my lines: "Let's talk
about it." "Things will look better in the morning." "I
understand how you must feel!"

Although I actually say and do what I visualized maybe
40 percent of the time, the atmosphere in our home is
usually much better than it was when I was just "doing what
comes naturally."

Self-programming is a way of creating yourself and of
developing chosen characteristics within yourself.

Besides self-programming, there is another inner thing
we need to do, and that is to search for and accurately
identify the things that are already inside us . . . to find and
feel our truest nature, our deepest beliefs, our best ideas.
Doing so requires solitude, and solitude in today's world is
surprisingly hard to find. As an urban society we are constantly around other people, and in the rare moments when
we could be alone, we turn on the television and resur-
round ourselves.

To find solitude, we sometimes have to go to the desert
or the mountains or the sea. Or we have to get up early in

the morning or stay up late into the night. But there is a rest and a rejuvenation in solitude that makes it worth whatever effort it takes or whatever schedule it requires.

Self-programming and visualizing are ways to alter who we are. Perhaps an even deeper need is to *discover* who we are. Self-discovery occurs in solitude. It is easier to find ourselves when we are alone, and to find the best and clearest (and most unique) thought that is in us. It has been said that "genius is alone."

One who thinks alone will gain ideas that are new—or at least ideas that are his or her own. And whether or not the thoughts are unique, they will be original and fresh and very likely understood or expressed in a brand-new way.

At a dinner party a friend posed an interesting question: Why were there so many original thinkers, so many great men of ideas and clarity and philosophical courage 250 years ago as this country was born? The population of the country was tiny, yet more great individuals seemed to emerge in that era than they do today from our vastly larger population. Some suggested that it may have been the historical challenges of the times and that much of it may have been the inspiration of God. But others wondered if it was the privacy and solitude those times afforded that gave individuals the time and the opportunity to think on their own and to explore and extend their ideas in the quiet clarity of their own minds.

Today, because of our urban lifestyle and our ever-present print and electronic media, we are surrounded and bombarded by the thinking of others—to the extent that any ideas we have feel a little secondhand, a little brain-stormed or overcooked, a little homogenized by the mixing, sloshing, and blending of the education and communication systems around us.

A quiet mind, alone, uninterrupted, uninfluenced by outside clatter or the perspectives of others, is a fertile seedbed for new thought—and for thoughts that perhaps could grow nowhere else.

Get away. Find both a time and a place for solitude and go there regularly if not often. Bring along a journal and a pen. Look inside yourself and inside your mind, and make some notes on what you find there.

The combination of self-programming and solitude can unlock the deepest parts of ourselves and energize our relationships with ourselves and with those around us.

Reserved "Relationship" Time

One way to avoid the neglect of important relationships is to make some standing appointments that never change.

Instead of giving our families (and ourselves) only our "leftover time"—only the bits of time that don't happen to be taken up by work and other demands—we need to block out some "prime time" which is only for relationships. Think about the possibilities on the following list and either adopt some of them or design some for yourself. Clearly no one can implement the whole list—just pick one or two that you like, or use the list to stimulate a better idea for yourself.

• *"Tuck-in time."* Often the best time to communicate with smaller children (adolescents, too, for that matter . . . the later it is, the more they will talk) is at bedtime. It's a natural time to talk about the day just past—its problems, their feelings. Set aside a certain number of nights each week to do the tucking in.

• *Dinner hour.* Traditionally the dinner table has been the place of family communication. The day's events were discussed and shared. What was common "then" is uncommon now. Families rarely eat together. Fast foods and busy schedules have turned eating into a process of quick "refueling." Change it back! Set aside at least one night a week—more if you can—when you will eat together as a family. Sit down and eat . . . and talk.

• *Each end of sleep.* Early morning is a beautiful and magnificent time that most people either sleep through or hurry through. And the still, late hours of evening that can be so thoughtful and reflective are too often spent passively in front of a TV. Learn to view the late and early moments as *your* time—your time to meditate, read, ponder, plan, pray—your time to improve your relationships with self and with God.

• *Sundays.* The notion of a sabbatical—of one time period in every seven that is used for rethinking and as a change of pace—is a clear and valid concept. But Sundays have become the day of the big game or the big party or the big outing. Change your definition of Sunday recreation— make it mean "re-creation." Set aside time to think, to reflect, to rest, and to work on relationships with your family and with your inner self.

• *The weekly date.* If you're married, continue your courtship by reserving one night each week for a date. (If your schedule won't allow a night that often, go for the British concept of a fortnight—every two weeks.)

• *The five-facet review.* As discussed earlier, if you have a family, use your weekly date once a month as a time to go to a quiet restaurant and discuss your children. Conduct a five-facet review of each child by asking yourselves, "How is Johnny doing physically? Mentally? Emotionally? Socially? Spiritually?" Take notes. Pick out one or two areas where you need to concentrate your parenting during the month ahead.

• *Transition time.* The time when you come home from work and enter your home is the key transition of the day. Instead of bringing the cares and frustrations of work in with you, you want to leave them behind and focus on relationships, especially during the first few minutes after you arrive. Pause before you enter your home. Make the transition mentally. Decide in advance to walk in and be totally *with* your family.

• *Family night.* Reserve one night a week (or one each fortnight) to do something with your family. Regard it as almost sacred, and don't let anything allow you to ignore or forget it. Don't let yourself rationalize your way out or give up. The activity, depending on the age of your children, can be anything from having ice cream together at home, to holding a family council, to teaching the children a lesson you want them to hear, to attending a basketball game or the ballet. The memories become deposits in the "emotional bank account" you share with family members— extending future trust and communication.

• *Morning devotional.* Get up early enough to spend ten or fifteen minutes together as a family before or during breakfast and before leaving for work or school. Read scripture and hold family prayer if you have religious convictions. If not, spend a few moments reading literature together or memorizing whatever you deem to be motivational and insightful, and discuss plans and goals for the day.

Whichever ideas or methods you try, remember that your time is yours. Before you give it away to the world, take some select little bits of it out—and set them aside. Reserve them for relationships.

Morality and Practicality

A television correspondent who had recently completed an in-depth report on the spread of AIDS was asked for his personal bottom-line conclusion. "This is a case," he said, "where traditional morality and simple practicality run exactly parallel."

Question: Doesn't traditional morality *always* run parallel to practicality? Aren't the basic values that we call traditional morality the most practical, safe, dependable, and happy guidelines that have ever been devised for how we should live?

I (Richard) have an acquaintance who is a highly trained, high-priced psychiatrist, and a very competent and caring person. A few years ago he was attending a church where the congregation's leader was a lay minister who was, by profession, a plumber.

Over the course of several months the psychiatrist observed that several of his patients were members of the same church and were also going to the lay minister for guidance. He also observed, to his dismay, that these people seemed to be benefiting more from the plumber-minister's free advice than they were from his costly consultation. (He didn't just observe it—several of them told him so and canceled their future appointments.)

He finally went to the minister and asked him to reveal the secret of his success in counseling and helping troubled people. The plumber answered, "Why, it's easy, really. I just talk with them until I find out which of God's commandments they're breaking—and then I tell them to stop."

Christians and Jews may call their values the Ten Commandments. Taoists may call theirs the Way. Buddhists, Hindus, and members of Islam have their own names for remarkably similar codes of conduct and values. Atheists and agnostics, while not ascribing the principles to Deity, nonetheless usually adopt philosophies that embrace similar rules of conduct and comparable basic values.

So whether our source is religion or philosophy or plain personal logic, the directions are similar if not identical. They are directions of honesty; of courage; of respect for life, property, family, and the commitments of marriage; of unselfishness and caring for one another; of setting aside some time for worship, meditation, or solitude; of avoiding greed and jealousy; and of self-reliance, discipline, and personal responsibility.

Traditional morality and *universal values* are interesting terms. They suggest that both logic and history teach us that certain ways of thinking and behaving work better than their alternatives.

The fact is that a moral lifestyle works better than any other lifestyle. The fact is that traditional morality always runs parallel both to practicality and to happiness. And many would go farther and say that immoral or amoral lifestyles always lead to some form of unhappiness or some kind of sickness—either physical, mental, or emotional.

The irony is that we live in a country with Judeo-Christian origins and orientation where eight out of the ten biblical commandments are broken (or badly *bent*) routinely—usually without guilt and without thought. (Think how little we live—and how little social credibility we give to—the commandments relating to the Sabbath day, to chastity and fidelity, to truly honoring our parents, to coveting, to dishonesty, to taking the Lord's name in vain, i.e., swearing, cursing—to putting "other gods" ahead of God, and to "worshiping" the idols and images of our world more than Deity.) What if these commandments are loving counsel from a wise Father? What if they are "the ten best ways to be happy"?

We are better at professing morality and traditional values than we are at living them, and we live in a society where people are looking for happiness in all the wrong places—and not finding it.

But, thank God, we also live in a society where we are free to choose our own lifestyles, our own priorities, our own morality. And despite its absence in most popular movies, music, and media, a substantial majority of Americans still subscribe to "traditional morality"—and try to live a life of discipline and correct priorities.

The case that is made for traditional values and morality is often religious or "preachy" in its tone and wording. And the case against them is often based on arguments of freedom and individual choice. Overlooked is the aspect of practicality and the commonsense conclusion that we ought to be willing to learn from the collective experience of every generation of humanity that has preceded us.

Whether we are religious believers or not, ignoring the

established values, morality, and "commandments" of history and society, and relying instead on our own experience, is the moral equivalent of rediscovering the wheel.

When we try to be completely objective and practical about the whole thing, it may come down to something as basic as time—and the fact that we each have a limited amount of time in our lives. During a lifetime we may have long enough to learn the truth and validity of a lot of principles for ourselves—by trial and error—but if we spend our lives learning lessons in this way, we will have time for little else, and we will suffer through more unhappiness and heartache than is necessary.

The meaning and validity of basic moral values are not vague or mysterious. They are about as obvious and straightforward as cause-and-effect can be. If we honor our parents, we create happiness both for them and for us. If we rest and renew ourselves on Sunday, we are better off for it. If we do not worship things other than God, and if we avoid jealousy and coveting, it will help us steer clear of the selfishness and greed that guarantee unhappiness. If we respect other people's lives and property, we will also respect ourselves more, and others will return our respect. And if we honor our marriage vows, we will create a deeper, more fulfilling, and more lasting partnership with our spouse.

If there is an underlying guideline or objective for this book, it is to propose solutions that work and that create happiness. Nothing qualifies more as a true solution, nothing has been proven to "work" more often, nothing has more consistently prevailed against unhappiness, and nothing gives a person more freedom from personal crisis and thus more time to pursue his gifts and develop himself than simple acceptance of and allegiance and adherence to what we have come to call traditional moral values.

Feelings and Honesty

Unexpressed feelings never die, they just get buried and come forth later in uglier forms.

There are two fundamental keys in all deep and genuinely beneficial relationships. One is empathy and the other is honesty. Unfortunately we sometimes operate under the confused notion that the two are incompatible. Empathy means being sensitive to the other person's feelings. If our own honestly expressed feelings are upsetting to the other person, we reason, then expressing them would not be empathetic.

It all depends on the type of relationship we are dealing with—and on the kind of relationship we want it to become. For the sake of simplicity, let us categorize relationships into two groups: (a) family or other important, deep, long-term relationships, where the goals are trust, mutual sharing, useful feedback, and sometimes even oneness; and (b) shorter-term, more-superficial relationships in business or "incidental life" where the goals are not to rock the boat and to avoid friction, differences, and hurt feelings.

In a B-type relationship the old adage "Some things are better left unsaid" is a wise guideline. In an A-relationship, this cliché is a slow-acting but deadly poisonous pill. It may be true that some hurtful, critical comments are best left unsaid during a moment of anger, but real feelings cannot go unsaid too long before they begin to fester and grow uglier than they originally were.

Often we make the mistake of confusing the objectives of a B-relationship with the objectives of an A-relationship. Avoiding conflict should not be the goal of an A-relationship. Rather the goal is to grow individually and collectively by reasoning together, learning from each other, sometimes through debating and resolving conflict.

When we were first married, I (Linda) assumed that the best thing to do when I was upset or angry was to try to forgive Richard of his shortcomings and muffle my anger. Luckily he figured this out when I started slamming drawers. When asked what was wrong, I would icily retort, "Nothing!" After a short time Richard convinced me that he really wanted to know. The first thing I remember telling him was that it drove me crazy that he had to eat a fourth meal in bed every night at eleven o'clock, particularly when he could make soft pizza sound like celery. "It's especially annoying," I said, "when I'm on a diet and starving to death and you're chewing away on food that smells divine!" (Richard agreed to stick to as quiet and as nonaromatic food as possible.)

As the years have passed, I have become so good at expressing my feelings that I think Richard regrets having ever taught me. Several times he has mentioned that he still likes me to tell him how I feel but that it would be great if I could do so with a little less aplomb! Our little hurt feelings and disagreements have sometimes brought about major wars, but they are short-lived—sometimes hours, sometimes days, but never weeks.

Partners in a relationship need to hold and express strong enough commitment and develop deep enough trust to allow them to accept and even welcome differences without worry or concern that the relationship is threatened. And they need to develop a time and place to clear the air, to honestly and candidly express their feelings, even when these feelings may be upsetting or unflattering to the other person, to be able to do so with full confidence that a meeting of minds can be reached.

Early in our marriage, partly because we were still learning to communicate (as we still are) and partly because our work and schooling separated us so often, Richard and I had some problems with unexpressed feelings that got buried and came forth later in uglier forms. We had started, by that time, the process of having Sunday sessions, a half hour individually to work on some plans for the coming week, followed by a meeting to work out our schedule together. One week, when we were both aware of some unexpressed feelings, we decided to add a little extra part to our meeting. We called it, for want of a better term, a feelings expression. The idea was to each take a few uninterrupted minutes and just express feelings to the other. I (Richard) remember our first one clearly because Linda started by telling me she loved, respected, and needed me. She then told me of two times during the past week when she had been very upset at me but hadn't found a way or a time to tell me about it. Because there was a spirit of commitment and love and because the feelings were expressed in the context of our private meeting, I was able to accept the implied criticism.

In turn, after expressing my love to Linda, I shared a couple of things that had bothered me. It cleared the air. We both felt better. So we adopted the idea, decided never to let anything fester for more than a week, and began to hold a short "feelings expression" each week as part of each Sunday session.

Do we really need a time and place—a "meeting"—little private speeches to each other to express our feelings? Of course we don't—not all the time. Feelings get expressed every day in all kinds of ways. But *sometimes* we *do* need it. One real "appointment to communicate" each week is not too much.

Decide which of your relationships are A-relationships. Within them commit yourself to full disclosure of feelings. Do not share selectively, share totally. Find ways that work for you—ways of expressing and uncovering your feelings rather than burying them.

Seeing Beyond Eyesight and the Power of Questions

The most important relationship of all is vertical rather than horizontal. And it involves gratitude, humility, wonder, and awe.

President Theodore Roosevelt, affected occasionally by feelings of importance and indestructibility, often invited his friend, the eminent naturalist William Beebe, to be an overnight guest at the White House. Their habit was to walk out onto the west balcony at dusk and watch the oncoming night and the emergence of the stars. As they appeared, Beebe would name them and tell Roosevelt their size and how many light-years they were away from the earth.

At a certain point he would say, "See that faint spot of light mist just beyond the lower left corner of the great square of Pegasus? It looks like a dim star, but it is actually the great spiral galaxy of Andromeda. It is as large as our

Milky Way galaxy, which contains every star we can see. Andromeda is seven hundred and fifty thousand light-years away and contains a hundred billion stars. And it is only one of hundreds of millions of galaxies. You and I, Theodore, are two small specks on one tiny planet that orbits one of the hundred billion stars in one of the hundreds of millions of galaxies."

At that point, Roosevelt would say, "I think we feel small enough now, William. Let's retire."

We are small. We live in a vast universe that is beyond our comprehension. In our tiny proportions even this one small planet is vast.

From the very beginning of understanding, man has pondered the vastness of earth and the incredibly greater vastness of the universe, we have considered the overwhelming organization of it all, and generally taken it as an indication, if not a proof, of a greater intelligence, of a power infinitely beyond man's.

But if there is compelling evidence of deity, it lies less in the incomprehensible bigness of things than in the intimate smallness of what happens inside of us in quiet moments when we are alone but do not feel alone.

Irrespective of people's religion (or their lack of it), most have concluded (or realized) that there are sources of knowledge or of insight other than the five senses. Buddhists call our inner perceptions the eye of truth, or the eye of soul. Rumi, the great Persian poet, wrote of "the eye of the heart . . . of which these two sensible eyes are only the gleaners." Saint Augustine said that "our whole business in this life is to restore to health the eye of the heart by which God may be seen."

From where does our "beyond senses" insight come? Is

it a product of our mind's ability to link together subconscious data, to recall consciously forgotten information
drawn from some universal intelligence? Or does it come to
us (or into us) from an external and higher intelligence and
a greater power than man?

It is a personal question and requires a personal answer
that everyone must find for himself. Regardless of how you
answer it, the next question is *how to tap in*, how to obtain
extrasensory insight into things such as self, purpose, direction, and meaning.

The "tapping in" question is a fascinating one because
the answer is a question. The way to connect, the way to get
the answers, is to ask the *questions*. Ask who you are. Ask
where you came from. Ask why you are here. Ask what you
should be doing with your life. Ask if there are better places
for you than where you are now. Ask big questions and
small questions. Ask questions even when you have no idea
where to look for the answers. *Ask even if you are unclear
about just whom you are asking.*

We live in an age that is oriented too much to answers
and not enough to questions. A truly educated man or
woman is not one with all the answers but one who knows
how to ask the right questions. Questions are not a sign of
weakness or doubt. They are a sign of the deepest kind of
security, and they are the trigger if not the source of the
most important and the most personal information and
insight we will ever get.

If you believe in God, direct your questions to him, for it
is only logical that (a) he knows the answers; (b) he would
like you to have at least some of them; and (c) he understands, whether you do or not, the means whereby he can
give them to you.

If you don't believe, ask the questions of yourself. In the first case the process is prayer, in this case the process is meditation. In both cases chances of an answer exist only when the questions have been asked.

Keep track of the insight questions you ask (of God or of yourself). Write them in a journal, jot them down during Sunday sessions. Refer back to them often. Re-ask them often. Occasionally you will return to a question and find, to your delight and perhaps to your surprise, that it has become an answer.

Implementing Goal Balance

"Two-Edged Goals" and "Relationship Bands"

Two Final New Habits

As with the other two forms of balance, the principle or theory of goal balance is easier to accept than it is to implement. While we know that people are more important than things, that relationships ultimately matter more than achievements, that what happens on the inside of our homes and the inside of ourselves counts more than what happens on the outside—while we *know* this, we often do not *live* it.

The creation and pursuit of *balanced* relationship and achievement goals is as difficult and demanding as it is rewarding. What it takes, like the other two forms of balance, is a weekly habit and a daily habit.

We call the weekly habit two-edged goals. Like a two-edged sword, two-edged goals cut both ways. They carve out achievement and accomplishment on one side; and they shape better relationships on the other side.

The habit is a simple one. During your weekly Sunday session, spend equal time on L-goals and on R-goals (see page 146). List the things you want to accomplish during the week, then think equally hard and equally long about the key relationships in your life and how you *want them to be*. In your first few Sunday sessions write out some "future-relationships descriptions" (see page 149). After they are written, simply spend a little time each Sunday reviewing them, perhaps adding something. As you review these descriptions or relationship goals each Sunday, they will feel more and more real and you will find the actual relationships of your life gradually and steadily conforming to what you have described.

The daily part of the habit is equally simple. Use a highlighter or nonpenetrating felt-tip marker to make three side-to-side "relationship bands" across your daily planner or schedule. Put one band across the very top, one across the very bottom, and one about two-thirds of the way down the page.

These relationship bands represent the "reserved time" discussed on pages 166–169—time that is reserved for the important relationships of life. The top band is the early-morning time that can be so powerful in strengthening our relationship with God, with family, and with self. It might be used for meditation, for scripture or prayer, for seeking beyond-senses insight (see pages 176–179), for self-programming (see pages 160–166), or perhaps in the effort to prioritize and give up things mentally (see pages 150–154). Or it might be used to gather as a family for a calm moment of prayer or reading before everyone goes his or her own way. The middle band is the dinner hour, or the transition time when you come home from work. (For a woman whose current career is her home, the transition time would be when the children come home from school.) It is time set aside to listen, to ask, to communicate, to find out all you can about what each other feels and thinks and needs; a few brief moments set aside, without things to do, when you are just there for those you love, for those who may need you.

The last band, at the end of the day, might be for your marriage relationship—a time to talk, to plan the next day together, or to openly discuss feelings. It might also be a time for important relationships with friends—to visit, to make a phone call. It might be a time to tuck a child into bed or to listen to an adolescent when he comes in late in the evening.

The important thing about relationship bands is that they are *reserved*. You quit thinking about things and quit worrying about what needs to be done during these brief (usually ten to fifteen minutes) interludes, and you focus on relationships and on the people who are closest to you. These reserved times can be flexible in length—perhaps a longer one some evening as you tuck children into bed and tell stories or in the afternoon transition time after a particularly hectic day—perhaps shorter on a night when all there is time for is a long look in the eyes, a pat on the head, and a sincere "I love you," or a busy early morning when all there is time for is a few deep breaths and a kind word or compliment for your spouse as you leave. The important thing is that whether they are short or long, the relationship bands happen—every day.

THE

System

What Does It Take?

Take a stand!

That is what you must do if you want Lifebalance.

If you want to swim your own course rather than being swept along by the world's currents, if you want to judge yourself by your own definition of success, if you want to make what you do match what you believe, then you must take a personal *stand*.

Hopefully some of the suggestions in this book will help you *design* and *implement* the stand you take.

Please don't get the idea from the personal illustrations in many chapters that the Eyres have achieved total Lifebalance. Naturally we've used our most positive experiences as examples. (Selectivity is one of the pleasures and prerogatives of authors.) We have made a strong commitment to the idea of Lifebalance, and it has changed the way we think and the way we live. But we certainly haven't arrived.

The point is that we never do, you never do, no one ever does! Lifebalance is a journey, not a destination. It is a worthwhile, rewarding, ongoing *struggle,* and often what we are struggling against seems to be the world around us—the norms, the "usual," the expected.

Before you totally commit to taking your own stand, you should know three things that the stand requires:

1. *Commitment:* To a new pattern of daily thinking and planning wherein you ponder the three balance points and

what you *choose to do* about each of them *before* you think
about your schedule and what you *have to do* that day.

2. *Awareness:* An effort to take off the blinders and see
and feel and *notice* more, and a willingness, even an anx-
iousness, to break your schedule and leave your list when
you notice something more important or more beautiful.

3. *Time:* A few minutes every day to "work the triangle,"
to draw the "serendipity line" and record the serendipities,
and to just be there during the "relationship bands." And a
half hour every Sunday ("the saw sharpening") to think
ahead through setting two-edged goals and to think back
through right-brain retention.

A Triangular Model for Balance

The symbol of a corner-nesting triangle split by a vertical line represents the three types of balance that we have discussed. Whether or not you use the "Lifebalance system" outlined in the following pages (and made available in greater detail and with "tools" on the last page of this book), the symbol will serve as a summary.

As mentioned earlier, a triangle is a figure or symbol of balance. It has no opposite corners, each line is connected to each other line, and like a tripod it will balance and sit solidly on uneven ground.

The three priorities we all try to balance (family, work, and self) are the three corners or balance points of the triangle. View the diagram as three separate "corners" pushed together so that they nest within one another.

The left corner represents work or career and is the outer figure in the logo since it occurs outside the home, or at least is external to the family itself.

The right, family corner nests mostly inside because it deals with things inside the home. And the self or character corner is deep within the symbol because it represents what is inside of us. The three priorities or corners can be referred to respectively as the outer, the inner, and the inner-inner.

The thin vertical line drawn through the triangle represents balance between the structure and scheduling of the left hemisphere of the brain and the spontaneity and serendipity of the right brain. This is the balance between acting and responding, between getting there and enjoying the journey. And it is often the balance between achievements and relationships, between things and people.

Note how the different types of balance come together in the symbol. The reason that the left "outer" corner of the triangle falls to the left of the center line is that, in most cases, work is a left-brain function and deals with achievement-type goals (or L-goals). However, a portion of this corner extends across to the right of the line, because relationships and spontaneity should also be a part of work.

Family is represented by the inner, *right* corner of the triangle because families are mostly a question of relationships, responding to needs, and using the spontaneous, flexible right hemisphere of the brain. Part of the corner crosses to the left side, however, since families do need some structure and some achievement goals, and since they are supported and sustained by work.

The top (and inner-inner) corner of the triangle symbolizes the self—the heart—the character that should be equally balanced between the structure, planning, and achievement of the left and the serendipity, flexibility, and relationships of the right.

It is important, if you choose to get into the Lifebalance system that follows, to keep in mind the meaning of the symbol and the three types of balance it represents. Whatever level of planning and balance we are discussing (day-balance, monthbalance, yearbalance, etc.), we will be dealing with all three corners or balance points and with both the "structured left" and the "flexible right."

Lifebalance

A Nine-Step System for Getting Yourself Balanced

Balancing is a process that is best worked into through a sequential, nine-step system that can change the patterns of how we think. Each step is named after the concept on which it is built. Basically the Lifebalance system is simply an organized, nine-step sequence for implementing the kind of balancing and "antiplanning" that this book has advocated.

Because the techniques involved in each of the nine steps have already been mentioned earlier in the book, this system provides a summary as it puts the steps together in the order that lends itself best to implementation. The system also gives us a chance to illustrate further some of the concepts mentioned earlier and to see them in a more practical, "implementable" light.

Please remember several things as you go into this system:

First, remember that Lifebalance intentionally comes with a little of its own terminology and jargon. Terms such as *serendipity line* or *balance points* not only make it easier to explain the system, they become part of our vocabulary and remind us and motivate us to stay with it and make it work. Each of the nine steps is named with one of the new

Lifebalance terms, and each step begins with a brief definition and review of its new term.

Second, remember that we sometimes refer to the Lifebalance system as *antiplanning* because it is designed to pull in a direction opposite from that of most time management. It provides a basic grid of structure and goals, but it pulls toward flexibility and spontaneity, toward family, relationships, and inner growth, and away from the more common time-management notion that the way to be successful is to do more things, be more efficient, waste less time, fill up every minute. Lifebalance and antiplanning are more in harmony with the ancient Oriental saying "To the noble art of getting things done we must add the more noble art of leaving things undone." Lifebalance attempts to increase not the quantity but the quality of the things we do.

Third, remember that the old bad habits of unbalance can be broken only by substituting the new good habits of balance. We said earlier that systems were part of the problem, but we were speaking of highly structured list-making systems that rob us of spontaneity and sensitivity. The unbalanced habits of bad systems can be broken (replaced) with the balanced habits of a good system.

Lifebalance is not a detail-oriented, mind-occupying scheduling system. Rather it is a priority-oriented, mind-freeing program of simplification that helps people implement the three kinds of balance discussed in this book. Most of the steps in the program are just basic good habits.

Fourth, remember that the steps we are going to present are not the only ways or necessarily the best ways to implement balance. You may develop your own way. Please don't feel threatened by a step-by-step system—and don't feel restricted or compelled by it. You've already read the ideas and content of the book. This last section doesn't contain any additional philosophy—just a summary of what we've said already, in the form of a program for simplifying and practicing the concepts of Lifebalance. We've already covered the *principles*. What's left to review is the *procedures*.

Conscientiously implemented, step 1 will bring about noticeable improvements in balance. Each successive step will enhance and add to that balance. The first four steps have to do with daily balance. The fifth step involves weekly balance, which can become a framework or guide for daily balance. The sixth and seventh steps develop monthly balance, which in turn makes the weekly balance more in tune and connected. Steps 8 and 9 deal with longer-range balanced goal setting, which provides "targets" at which we can aim our monthly and weekly balance.

STEP 1. BALANCE POINTS: The three areas of life (work, family, and self) that need daily attention if balance is to be obtained.

The first step is to decide and to commit. Decide personally to adopt the goal of balancing *family* with *self* with *work*. Commit to making yourself do the hard mental effort that is required to bring about this balance.

The first step in changing our thought is to change what we think *about*. Simply by adopting the conscious goal of building our lives solidly on all three balance points, we begin to re-form our thought patterns and readjust where we spend our mental energy.

STEP 2. PRIORITY BLANKS: The three daily choose-to-dos that are filled in on the three lines at the top of the

planning page each day *before* any scheduling is done—one line for each of the three balance points. The process of deciding on the single most worthwhile thing you can do each day for each balance point is called *working the triangle*.

Think of a day as a blank piece of paper.

The day is tomorrow. It's close, it's almost here, but it hasn't started yet. So it's blank, clean, undetermined. What do you want to write on your day?

What is important to you? What should you write on that day for yourself before you show it to the world, before you give it to others and let them start deciding where you will be, what you will do, whom you will see, how you will spend your time?

Before you write anything, and before you think about what you have to do, or even about what you can accomplish, draw the three little horizontal lines (priority blanks) at the top of your page and ask yourself what is the single most important or meaningful thing you could choose to do that day in each of the three balance points of self, family, and work.

Many things may come to mind that you *have to do* in your job and for your family, but these must be choose-to-dos—based on perceived need rather than on mandated necessity. Think hard and focused for five minutes and look through your consciousness for one need for yourself,* one need for your family, and one need at work. Then write these three priorities, or choose-to-dos, on your three priority blanks.

When you have finished, the top of your page might look

---

* Remember that the area of self includes service to others as well as personal development of self.

something like this: (The three angles represent the three balance points or corners of the triangle as explained on pages 187–188.)

∧	Do Aerobics
>	Discuss "Boy Problem" with Lisa
<	Compliment Sally on Production Ideas

If you use a planner or time-management tool, draw your three priority blanks in at the top of each day and think about them *before* dealing with the details, commitments, and schedule of the day. If you don't use a planner, put your priority blanks on a plain sheet of paper.

Try it for twenty-one days. Some of the things you write on your priority blanks may be very small things ("Compliment Bill on yesterday," "Take solitude walk," "Call Wendy"), but they are things you consciously decided were important on one of your balance points. After twenty-one days you'll have formed a habit, and the cumulative effect of your choose-to-dos will be evident to you—twenty-one specific things you have done for someone in your family, twenty-one things you have done for yourself, and twenty-one thoughtful but nonrequired things you did at work.

After twenty-one days you will have at least the beginnings of a new habit of balance, and you will be ready to go to step 3.

STEP 3. RELATIONSHIP BANDS: Small segments of each day that are reserved for relationships; *transition* *times* **during the day when one consciously focuses on the needs of people rather than on the accomplishments of things; short, regular periods to just be there for those you love.**

The three most effective times to think about the important relationships of our lives are during the three transitions that each day contains—early morning as we get up, late afternoon or early evening when we return from work, and late evening at bedtime. Step 3 is a decision to concentrate exclusively on relationships during these three transition times.

Use a highlighter or nonpenetrating marker to make three "relationship bands" or spaces across each day—one early in the morning, one late in the evening, and one around dinnertime—reserved spaces where you will work on relationships instead of on achievements. The bands reserve or set aside a little time early in the morning for meditation or planning or maybe a family prayer; a little debriefing time after work or after school when you ask questions of interest and concern, shift gears from the concerns of your job, and get your mind on the people you live with; and a little time in the evening, perhaps for tucking children into bed or talking with your spouse or calling a friend. The bands only take up a few minutes of the day, but if you don't put them on your days before you start scheduling, the time will get swallowed up by the less important details, errands, and have-to-dos.

It's not necessary to write anything in the bands—nor to plan anything specific for them. Just reserve the time for yourself and your family, to enjoy the moments together and to tend to whatever needs come up.

A daily page, altered to include both priority blanks and relationship bands, will look something like the next page in this book.

Try step 3 for twenty-one consecutive days. You will find that the transition times, reserved by the relationship bands, become the most relaxing as well as the most rewarding parts of your day. When the habit is formed and you have felt the power and cumulative effect of these brief, reserved moments, move on to step 4.

STEP 4. SERENDIPITY LINE: A top-to-bottom line placed on a daily schedule to separate the "planned things" on the left from the spontaneous opportunities and needs that cannot be planned on the right. *Serendipity* **means the ability, through awareness and flexibility, to find something good while seeking something else; and** *jumping the line* **refers to the process of being aware enough and flexible enough to notice the serendipity side of life and to jump across to something spontaneous and unplanned two or three times each day.**

Code the pages of your life by drawing a vertical line right down the center of each day and labeling the right-hand side "Serendipity." Write your schedule on the left, leaving the right-hand side blank—as a reminder to stay aware, to stay observant, to keep the blinders off, and to notice happy surprises, unexpected opportunities, new acquaintances, unplanned needs, and anything and everything else that could not have been planned or scheduled.

Commit yourself to jumping over the "spontaneity line" at least a couple of times during the day in an effort to keep yourself awake and flexible and to keep things exciting.

∧	Do Aerobics
>	Discuss "Boy Problem" with Lisa
<	Compliment Sally on Production Ideas

A fully "coded" antiplanning page incorporating priority blanks, relationship bands, and the serendipity line will look something like the next page in this book.

Most planning starts with scheduling and with a quick listing of demands, commitments, and have-to-dos. Things such as family, personal needs, and relationships are left off or left until last. And spontaneity is killed, buried under the heaviness of "the list."

With antiplanning, the process is reversed. We start with our priority lines, relationship bands, and serendipity line, committing ourselves to them *before* we start listing things. Then, when we do write our schedule, it might look something like the page after next in this book. (Depending on your own preferences and style, you may make a list as detailed as the one that follows, or you may do a much simpler list.)

Note that the three priorities (choose-to-dos) got onto the schedule. They always will once the three priority blanks identify them and recognize them. They seldom will if you just start *scheduling* and *doing* without *thinking*.

Note also that nothing is written on the serendipity side nor in the relationship bands. Don't plan things for these spaces. Instead train yourself to be more aware . . . of people, of situations, of need, of beauty, of opportunity. When your awareness shows you something more worthwhile than what you'd planned to do, be flexible enough (and brave enough) to jump over the line and do it.

Jot down the serendipity things and the relationship things as they happen or *after* you do them. You are writing them down not as a plan or a schedule but as a *result*—as a good memory and as a compliment to yourself for noticing them and choosing them.

∧ Do Aerobics

> Discuss "Boy Problem" with Lisa

< Compliment Sally on Production Ideas

Serendipity:

∧ Do Aerobics

\> Discuss "Boy Problem" with Lisa

\< Compliment Sally on Production Ideas

6:30 Up-ready
6:45 Aerobics, shower
7:30 Breakfast meeting
     (Sharon)
8:30 office
        - Bills
        - memoes
          (inc. Steve)
        - note to Sally
        - Phone calls
        - call Pete
        - confirm lunch
10:30 meeting-Production
11:30 Prepare arguments
      for Jim
12:45 Lunch-Pete
1:30 Plant inspection
2:30 Jim-win his approval
3:30 answer mail
      make sales follow up
5.   Pick up Lisa after
      school-talk

Serendipity:

6:30 Home-news-mail
7   Dinner w/Family

     call uncle Ben
     (how feeling?)

9:00 Johnson
     reception

By the end of the day your page might look like the next page in this book.

The day was rather well planned, but it didn't go exactly according to plan. The person in this example wasn't troubled by this fact—on the contrary. He chose to "jump the line" several times, either because circumstances prevented him from doing what he had planned or because something came up that was more important (or more worthwhile or more beneficial) than what he had planned. He was interrupted in the morning when Bill Alexander dropped by, and he could have just said a brief hello and gone back to his memo. But he sensed an opportunity and ended up talking to Bill for over an hour.

He had planned to eat with Pete, but when Pete couldn't go, he browsed the bookstore instead and noticed a book on houseboats that gave him an idea about how his family could achieve the "ultimate vacation" they had been talking about.

When his wife Patty was late getting home, instead of being upset that they wouldn't have dinner together, he started cooking and then let Lisa (with whom he had just finished a personal talk) finish the meal preparation while he took his youngest boy to the park for an hour.

Later that evening Billy had a problem with his homework that was more important than dropping by at a business reception as he had planned.

Note that when "serendipity things" have come up, they have been written in across the line, and things he decided not to do (in favor of the serendipity) have been crossed off. The crossing off doesn't mean he did them—it means he *didn't* do them . . . *chose* not to. Maybe tomorrow he will come back to some of them.

∧   Do Aerobics

>   Discuss "Boy Problem" with Lisa

<   Compliment Sally on Production Ideas

6:30   Up-ready
6:45   Aerobics, shower
7:30   Breakfast meeting
          (Sharon)
8:30   office
          - Bills
          - memoes
             (inc. Steve)
          - note to Sally
          - Phone calls
          - call Pete
          - confirm lunch
10:30 meeting - Production
11:30 Prepare arguments
          for Jim
12:45 Lunch-Pete
1:30   Plant inspection
2:30   Jim-win his approval
3:30   answer mail
          make sales follow up
5.   Pick up Lisa after
          school-talk

Serendipity:

Met Tom Alexander
with Apex-originally
from San Mateo –
married-2 kids –
interested in the
power project –
Secretary's name: Jan

Bookstore-found
     houseboat idea

changed strategy:
Got Jim's dept.
involved instead of
just "winning him
over"

6:30   Home-news-mail

7   Dinner w/Family

       call uncle Ben
       (how feeling?)

9:00   Johnson
          reception

Patty not home yet
Beautiful evening
Lisa volunteered to
start dinner. Took
little Joe to zoo for
an hour (Remember
his face when he
watched the Gibbon
monkeys "play tag")
Finished w/Billy on math-
got into discussion of
"what he wants to be"

Note also that what is written on the serendipity side and in the relationship bands is in the past tense. He didn't plan to talk about Billy's worries about his math test. What he did was save that time to listen and pay attention to people he cares about. Billy brought up the math test because he was listening. After the fact he wrote the incident in on the relationship band.

This is not to say that he didn't plan anything that has to do with relationships. Picking up Lisa and calling Uncle Ben were both things he decided to do as he thought about priorities. These things were scheduled—but not in the relationship bands. These bands are the few minutes set aside to listen and feel in the present tense—to be especially aware of the people you are with or thinking about that moment.

Steps 1–4. Fine-tuning the Process of Daily Balance

What is the best time for the "five-minute sit-there," for the pondering of choose-to-dos that precede scheduling? For some (the type of people who might be called larks), the best time is the first thing in the morning while the mind is fresh. For others (who might be called owls), the best time seems to be the late evening—looking ahead and thinking about tomorrow so that they can sleep on it.

Decide for yourself whether you are a lark or an owl. If you are not sure, experiment by trying it both ways.

You also need to make a decision about what type of schedule book you will carry. You will need to have a separate page for each day, and we suggest monthly booklets so that you will not be carrying something too big or too bulky. The other advantage of a monthly booklet is that you change books at the first of each month, which provides the kind of review that we suggest be a part of your Sunday session on the first Sunday of each month. Special monthly antiplanner booklets are available (see the last page of this book), or you may adapt any day-by-day schedule book simply by adding priority blanks, relationship bands, and serendipity lines.

So . . . there you have the daily process for balance. Now, the next thing we're going to tell you is that it has to be done every day, right? That you must never let a day go by without a "five-minute sit-there" . . . right?

Wrong. This is not some monastery you're entering—or some performance contract you are signing in blood. On the contrary, this is something you will do because you enjoy it, because it will add excitement to your life along with an extra measure of calmness and balance. Remember, it's rigid structure and the pressure of perfection that we're trying to get *away* from.

We suggest you don't fill out anything too specific on weekends. Let Saturday be a day to get away from goals, to do what comes naturally. You may need to make a list of household chores or errands, but keep it simple and easy. Use Sunday for rest, worship, and the kind of deeper reflection we've called saw sharpening.

The daily Lifebalance form we have illustrated is basically for weekdays. And even on weekdays, don't demand 100 percent perfection. If you miss a day—not holding a five-minute sit-there, not filling in the priority blanks, and so forth—don't worry about it. You'll still have the weekly balance form, which will be discussed next, and it may actually be good to miss a day once in a while as a change of pace.

Do try to be consistent, however, in daybalancing for the first few weeks (twenty-one days) on each new procedure to form the habit. After a few weeks you will be fully aware of the quality the process can add to your life. From then on you will use daybalance not because you have to but because you want to.

Daybalancing, and the effective use of priority blanks, relationship bands, and the serendipity line, can change the way you feel, the way you think, and the way you live. As you learn the art of working the triangle, jumping the line, and reserving time through relationship bands, you will develop a balance that will minimize stress and frustration even as it helps you accomplish more of what is meaningful.

As mentioned earlier, one of the first things you will notice and appreciate is that your definition of a perfect day will change. If (before Lifebalance) you were a structured person who made long lists and got your jollies by crossing things off your list as you did them (and when you did something not on your list, you quickly wrote it on so that you could cross it off) . . . if you were that kind of person, your definition of a perfect day will change from

"A day when I cross everything off"

to

"a day when I cross off the most important things but also have some spontaneous, unplanned happy accidents."

And if (before Lifebalance) you were an unstructured person who would usually go with the flow and do whatever came up or seemed most pressing at the moment . . . if you were that kind of person, your definition of a perfect day will change from

"a day when everything just seemed to go well"

to

"a day when I decided what was most important in the three areas of my life and *chose* to do them, and still had time for flexibility."

After you have changed your definitions and formed the habits of daybalancing, go on to step 5.

STEP 5. SUNDAY SAW SHARPENING: (Sunday sessions for weekbalancing): Taking a few minutes the first day of the week to decide what is most important during the seven days ahead.

Our mental saws need weekly sharpening!

The daily five-minute sit-there just discussed is definitely the key to daybalance, but it can't really qualify as saw sharpening. Genuine sharpening requires a longer period of deeper thought—at least a focused half hour at a set time each week. And the best time to do it is on the first day—on Sunday. Deciding in advance what you will try to do during the week ahead for each balance point will make daily balancing easier and more natural.

Set aside at least half an hour each Sunday to think about the week ahead. Once again, use the triangle model and think about your work, your family, and yourself, both in terms of what you need and in terms of what service you can give to others. Lay out or draw your week on a full sheet of paper.

As with daybalancing, avoid thinking first about what you have to do during the coming week. Think first about what is needed, about what you *want* to do and *choose* to do in each of the three priorities or balance points of life. *Then* (after thinking about the priority areas) begin to think about what you will do when and to consider each day of the week ahead.

The Sunday session example on the next page will help you to understand the concept of saw sharpening. Despite (or perhaps because of) its simplicity, this format can be of great assistance in balancing and prioritizing a week. The specific examples included may or may not fit your own situation or needs, but it will give you the idea.

The three balance points (work, family, and self) are represented by the three boxes at the top of the page. The work box appears on the left not because it is first but because it is usually a left-brain, achievement-oriented function. (See Lifebalance symbol and discussion on page 187.) The "self" balance point is in the middle because a balanced self requires equal emphasis on right-brain relationships and left-brain accomplishments. The family balance point is on the right because of the flexibility and right-brain insight that families require.

Setting up and using this type of form is simple. Write down, inside the three squares, the most important things you can do for each priority or balance point during the coming week. Put an open circle by each item you list (which you can color in to signify completion).

Box 1:
- Finish 1/3 of month's sales quota
- Improve relationship with Bart in shipping dept.
- move bank account - get on line
- Get car inspected
- Pay first of month bills

Box 2:
- Run 15 miles
- Read Scripture (15 chapters)
- "Day balance" everyday (work the triangle)
- Finish cancer drive assignment
- 1 hour of volunteer work at hospital

Box 3:
- Family outing (dinner and movie - celebrate first anniversary in house)
- Flowers or poetry to Patty
- Get in touch with Aunt Jane (help with her move?)
- Help Jim on 7-8-9 timetables
- Get together at least 3 nights
- Write letter to Lance in Switzerland

SUNDAY
- Read Scripture
- Church
- "Sunday Sessions"
- Family meeting (plan week together)
- Day balance

MONDAY	TUESDAY	WEDNESDAY	THURSDAY	FRIDAY	SATURDAY
Run 5 mi		Run 5 mi	call Aunt Jane (before 7:00)	Run 5 mi	Spring cleaning (yard)
WORK					Fishing with boys
Visit with Bart when I bring orders down	Change bank account	Final appointments to finish quote	12:00 car inspected	order flowers	
Family outing	Eat together Pay bills	Basketball Tickets	Eat together Cancer Drive	S. to piano lesson symphony	
Scriptures		Scriptures		scriptures	

Once again, it is important to do this *first*, before you begin to think about the schedule or requirements of the week ahead. The great failure or error of most typical weekly planning is that it begins with the listing of obligations and with filling up the time without any effort to consider what is most important. Then typically we finish that process and say to ourselves, *Busy week again—darn it—no time for family or personal needs.*

Weekbalance and the Sunday session *reverse* this process. You think first about the most important areas of life, and decide or choose what to do about each during the week ahead.

Then you use the little calendar below to jot down when you will do those priorities and to fit them in with the other obligations and schedules of the week ahead. Don't fill the calendar with details. You can save that for daybalance. Just use the calendar to decide when you will tend to your priorities and to block out a graphic overview of the week ahead.

You will find, when you take a full half hour in a Sunday session to think about your coming week, that your mind will identify for you what is important in each area. You will then find that, with your weekbalance complete, daybalancing during the week ahead will become both easier and more rewarding.

Hold Sunday sessions for three consecutive weeks. You will find an improvement in the quality of how you are spending your time, and your daily balancing flows from your Sunday plan (and adds up to its completion by the end of the week). When you feel comfortable with Sunday sessions, go on to step 6.

STEP 6. EXPANDED "FIRST SUNDAY" SUNDAY SESSION: An expanded Sunday session, held on the first Sunday of the month just past, creates in the mind a balanced view of the month ahead.

Just as daybalancing is aided by weekly goals, weekbalancing is assisted and made more effective by monthly goals and priorities.

The best time to think about the month ahead is in an expanded Sunday session on the first Sunday of each month or the last Sunday of the previous month.

The process is very similar to weekbalancing. Discipline yourself to think first about what you ought to do and choose to do during the month ahead in each of the three priority areas. Then fit these things in with the events and schedules for the month in the weekday and weekend spaces that take up the bottom of the page.

The example on the following page will help you design a simple form for your own monthbalancing. Notice that each week consists of a block for the five weekdays and a second, smaller block for the weekend. Note also that there is no effort to do any detailed planning—only to list the main activities and focus points for each week and to decide when the goals for each of the balance points above will be done.

STEP 7. RIGHT-BRAIN RETENTION: Keeping track of the ideas and insights that come spontaneously or in flashes, as well as the unexpected people, needs, and opportunities that cross one's life.

As you practice lifebalancing on a daily basis, you will accumulate, on the pages of your daily schedules, numer-

- Reach sales quota
- Invest 1/10 of month's income
- Look into possibility of trading car—make decision
- Proposal written for combining sales areas
- Get smoother cooperation with shipping dept.

- In training for 10 k race (27:00)
- Read three books from New Testament (Paul Epistle)
- Resume volunteer work
- Be up at 6 each day—have personal time before breakfast

- Get new back lawn put in back
- Improve order and neatness in home
- Individual "Daddy date" with each child

---

observe shipping order dept. start draft of proposal Family meeting on ORDER	Lisa's Daddy date	New grass-spring cleaning (yard & house) Sunday Scripture study	Run 15 mi
M - T - W (Detroit trip)	First half of sales quota final Billy's Daddy date	Weekend family trip Church	Run 15 mi
Locate investment options Decision on car	Tim's Daddy date	Volunteer work in Hospital Church	Run 15 mi
Finish sales quota, finish proposal	Thurs-Fri (sales convention in DePaul)	overnight camping Church	Run 15 mi

ous notes about ideas, people, and events that you want to retain and that you may wish to refer back to.

There will be times when you want to refer back to the left-side schedule—to recall when you did something or to review your activities for a specific day. In addition you will wish to refer to something on the right side of a particular day. And it will usually be an idea, a spontaneous event, or notes you made about a new person you met.

It gets harder and harder to find these notes as time passes—unless you keep a simple chronological index of the things you want to remember (see the next page).

Usually when you want to recall something, you have a pretty close idea of when it happened, so you can find it by checking your index for the period of time during which you think it occurred.

If you set up your index like the following example, then your date column will tell you when it happened, and how far across the page you make your entry will tell you whether it referred to an idea, an event, or a person.

At the end of a month (during your monthly "First Sunday" Sunday session), take the time to go back through the previous month's daily balance sheets and notes (or the daily pages in whatever kind of scheduling book you are using). When you come to notes on any event, idea, or person that you want to retain and have access to, enter it (with as few words as possible) on the right day and in the correct column of your idea index.

You will enjoy the right-brain retention process. It will refresh your memory and put things where you can find them. And it will allow you to relive the best moments of the month just passed.

Try the "First Sunday" Sunday session, complete with

Date:	Event:	Idea:	Person:
5-16	Incredible sunset - see poem		Tom Alexander- from San Mateo- 3 kids-Sec: Jan
5-17		Try backing up the reinforcement with the new adhesive from Syms	
5-19	Went to concert on impulse- <u>moved</u> by final concerto!		Took Billy to meet ball players at Park
5-20		Take whole family to new Caravelle campground some weekend	Anne Russell- Billy's math teacher-said we would call
5-22	Remarkable article in <u>Time</u> (see notes)	might want to look into Billows Co. as possible publisher for next training manual	

right-brain retention, for a couple of months. When you feel comfortable with them, go on to step 8.

Steps 1–7. A Small Investment of Time

Just in case (at first reading) steps 1 through 7 look time-consuming, please accept our promise that they are actually *timesaving*. Out of the 168 hours in a week, the Lifebalance system requires only 1 hour (five minutes per day for the "sit-there," and thirty minutes for the Sunday session). That 1 hour can dramatically increase the quality as well as the effectiveness of the other 167.

STEP 8. LONG-RANGE L-GOALS: Things one wants to achieve or accomplish during the next year (or longer). These goals of getting things done usually involve lists, logic, and the left brain, so we call them L-goals. The yearly day away is the day (ideally in a retreat setting) that is devoted to sorting out these balanced long-range L-goals.

Forming the habit of establishing a single priority each day for family, work, and self, using relationship bands, and developing the awareness that prompts regular jumping the line into serendipity will greatly increase a person's Lifebalance. And spending a few saw-sharpening moments every Sunday to set weekly and monthly goals as a target for the daily priorities to aim at will further enhance that balance.

Still, many people will want to go farther. They will want to know that their balancing is adding up to something larger and longer-range. They may worry that what they are planning each day and each week and each month is too often based on what is expected or required of them at the moment, rather than on what they choose or believe or want for themselves and for their lives.

Lifebalance reaches its purest form and produces its finest results (and its greatest joy) when daily and weekly prioritizing is backed up by balanced longer-range goals.

It is extremely hard mental work to establish yearly and

longer-range goals. Once they are set, however, Sunday sessions become far more effective, and daily and weekly balancing becomes part of a grand design.

Step 8 involves getting away for at least one full, uninterrupted day each year to project all three balance points into the future. Spend this yearly getaway in a place that is conducive to thought and meditation. Being away from home, office, and normal surroundings will sharpen your perspective.

Think with pencil in hand. Make notes, draw diagrams, doodle, dream a little. Deal with all three balance points. Arrange your goals around the three corners of the life-balance triangle. What do you want to accomplish over the next several years (and particularly during the coming year) in your work or career? What do you want to bring to pass in your personal life, within your own body and your own character? And what do you want to see happen in your family? How do your goals in each of the three areas relate to each other? What are the things you can do during the coming year that will really matter ten, or fifteen, or even twenty years from now?

Before your day away ends, try to simplify. Boil your thoughts down to a few clear goals for each balance point. Then look at the months of the year and make some decisions about when you will do what.

This type of thinking and projecting is fun and imaginative, but it is also difficult and mentally taxing. You may come home with a headache. But what an investment this day away can be. Once you have thought through the year ahead, you will have a course to follow, a track to run on, and a foundation and framework for monthly, weekly, and daily balancing all through the coming year.

STEP 9. LONG-RANGE R-GOALS: Goals that deal with people rather than things. These goals involve relationships and the intuitive right hemisphere of the brain, so they are called R-goals. When we set R-goals to do with our L-goals, we have created two-edged goals.

It is important to note that R-goals are very different from L-goals (just as relationships are different and require different things than achievements). But it is also important to realize that despite their differences L-goals and R-goals are very similar in terms of how they work. In both cases we have to be specific enough about our goals that we can literally see them as accomplished in our minds. Thus, with an L-goal, we write it down or list it and work until we can cross it off our list. With an R-goal, we write it down by *describing* in writing a relationship *the way we want it to be.* In either case what we have written is a mental conception of something that we then go out and (consciously and subconsciously) pursue and achieve.

R-goals are produced not through the logical or sequential analysis but through the kind of visualizing and imagining that you can do with your right brain.

The only way to get R-goals on paper is through description. Use part of your yearly day away to attempt to visualize as clearly as you possibly can the type of person you want to be in one year's time—and the kind of relationships you want to have by then. Then you describe your future self and your future relationships.

Begin with pen and paper by trying to describe the relationship you want to have with yourself at the end of your year. (Your confidence, your self-talk, your character, your feelings.)

Then describe your future relationship with your spouse. Then with your children, then with your best friends. Don't worry too much about being realistic. After all, you are not describing what exists now; you are describing what you want to exist in the future, at the end of this year you are thinking through.

Remember the principle involved here. If you can clearly imagine and describe a much-improved relationship—if you can envision it in your mind—then you can obtain it. Your subconscious mind and the whole intuitive, magical right hemisphere of your brain will point you and propel you toward the actions and attitudes that will turn your description from a wish or a dream into reality.

A relationship description of "self" might start something like this:

> I have just turned thirty-eight years old and am feeling more secure about myself and more happy with my life than ever before. The job is good! I take excellent care of myself. Physically I am in much better shape than I was a year ago. I'm more observant and sensitive, and I seem to get more enjoyment from everyday life. . . . I am honest with myself, and I can admit that . . . etc.

A relationship description for a spouse might begin something like this:

> Patty is now thirty-six. We have been married now for fifteen years and are more in love than ever. We share every feeling and have thrown out the idea that some things are better left unsaid. We are true partners in that we plan together. We

respect and admire each other and appreciate our differences. We're learning to be patient and gentle with each other and to prioritize each other above everything else, even the children. We find that we can . . . etc.

Sometimes it is easier to describe a desired relationship by actually picking an event in the future, or a particular place and thing, and then describing a relationship on that day and in that place. For example, a relationship description with a son might start like this:

Tommy is now nine years old. It is the opening day of fishing season and we are alone together in the early morning, fishing on the sandy bank of the river. There is a real joy in being together. He knows how proud I am of him and I feel his pride in me. No subject is off-limits. He asks me about friends, about a problem in school, even about the facts of life. I'm always honest with him, and I always have time to listen. After he catches his first fish of the morning, he looks at me and says . . . etc.

When you get your R-goals descriptions the way you want them, put them with your L-goals and you will have the kind of two-edged goals that will serve as a framework for the balancing you will do in your weekly Sunday sessions during the coming year.

Epilogue

Tightrope walkers stroll along a high wire with the ease that most of us walk down the street. They do so with the aid of a balance bar—the long pole they carry that stabilizes and steadies their progress.

To stay steady and balanced on the tightrope of life, we need our own kind of balance bar—one made up of strong commitments to clear priorities and of thought patterns that focus both our plans and our sensitivity on the things that really matter.

Anwar Sadat once stated, "He who cannot change the very fabric of his thought will never be able to change reality."

No one changes the fabric of a person's thought but that person. Your balance bar, in other words, will have to be of your own making. But you may have found some of the building materials in this volume.

We were sitting and thinking together one day. It had been a couple of months since we had finished the manuscript for this book. We had set it on the shelf to simmer for a time so that we could read through and edit it with a fresh perspective.

When we read it again, something became very clear to us: *Balance is a formula for joy.*

When we are balanced, there is more satisfaction and pleasure in work and in the process of accomplishing things in the outside world. And balance, most importantly, brings with it the deeper joys that spring from what happens inside our homes and inside ourselves.

We've avoided the usually overused word *success* throughout this book, so let us use the word twice in this last section. *Lifebalance means balancing the outer success of work and career with the inner success of family and personal growth.*

While this is the end of a book, we hope that it is, for you, the beginning of a process—perhaps even the beginning of a *quest* for more quality and more balance in life.

Balance, like most other truly worthwhile things, is something we never fully perfect or completely attain. Rather it is something we can always be obtaining. The tightrope walker is never balanced in the sense of being still or stationary—he is always balancing, and gradually becoming better and more comfortable in his balance.

In reality, balancing is a skill that can become an art—an art we can master only when it is our conscious goal.

Follow-up

For some the book is enough. For others it isn't. If you want to get *farther* into Lifebalance—via materials and a program that walks you through the long and short-term goals that create a more balanced life—here is what's available:

- *Lifebalance "antiplanners"*
A set of twelve monthly antiplanner booklets with each daily page incorporating priority blanks, spontaneity lines, and relationship bands and with monthly and weekly spreads for laying out longer-term balance goals.

- *Lifebalance Seminars*
An eight-part, in-home Lifebalance Seminar (each part consisting of an audiotape and printed supplements, forms, and worksheets). The seminar includes the antiplanner booklets.

- *HOMEBASE Newsletter and Programs*
Ten issues per year, each containing new ideas and concepts of *Lifebalance* and methods for doing a better job with relationships and family. There are also three parenting programs available: *Teaching Children Values, Teaching Children Joy,* and *Teaching Children Responsibility.* Each program consists of audiotapes and/or workbook manuals for parents *and* kids.

- *Spiritual Serendipity*
A book by Richard that goes further into the spiritual aspects of *Lifebalance.*

For questions or further information on becoming a member of S.J.S. HOMEBASE or on any of the Eyres' books and programs on Lifebalance and parenting, call (801) 581-0112.

To order Lifebalance materials or supplies, call (800) 772-4859.

About the Authors

Richard and Linda Eyre were living the book *Lifebalance* long before they wrote it. Richard is a Harvard M.B.A. who runs several businesses, has twenty books in print, writes poetry, enters tennis and basketball tournaments, ran for governor, and has held several presidential appointments in Washington. Linda is a concert violinist, writer, teacher, and was named by the National Council of Women as one of America's six outstanding young women. The Eyres' book *Teaching Your Children Values* was a national New York Times #1 best-seller. They host a national cable TV show called *Families Are Forever* and two national satellite TV shows called *Teaching Your Children Values* and *Lifebalance* and have appeared on virtually every national and morning talk show from *Donahue* to *Oprah* and from *Today* to *CBS Good Morning*.

The Eyres' highest priority is their family, which consists of nine natural children plus a student from Bulgaria (not to mention the dogs, cats, gerbils, horses, and other residents). They alternate their residence between homes in Salt Lake City; Jackson Hole, Wyoming; and Washington, D.C.

Richard and his sons play on a basketball team called FFE (Future Fathers of Eyrealm), which plays in community and recreational leagues.

The Eyres don't believe anyone should pattern their life after theirs, but they do believe there is enough time to do a great many things and that everyone can find that time through his or her own form of Lifebalance.

ALSO AVAILABLE

If you have enjoyed *Lifebalance*, you'll want a copy of the following titles available at your favorite bookstore:

Teaching Your Children Values

The #1 national bestseller. A practical, proven, month-by-month program of games, family activities, and value-building exercises for kids of all ages.

Three Steps to a Strong Family

Named one of the best parenting books of the year by *Child* magazine. A three-step program for raising responsible children and making families flourish.

Teaching Your Children Joy

A book that will help you give your children the foundation they need to grow into positive and fulfilled adults.

Teaching Your Children Sensitivity

A practical volume of usable ideas for teaching sensitivity and service.

Teaching Your Children Responsibility

A simple, practical program with enjoyable exercises, games, and activities that you can use to teach your children these important concepts.

Don't Just Do Something, Sit There

In his wise, witty, and down-to-earth style, Richard Eyre challenges the "wisdom of the ages" by reshaping common cliches into inspiring thoughts relevant to the way we live now.

I Didn't Plan to Be a Witch
And Other Surprises of a Joyful Mother

A reassuring and hilarious report on being a mother in today's hectic world.